# PICTURES FROM AN EXHIBITION

# PICTURES
# FROM AN
# EXHIBITION

ED. PAUL KAVANAGH

THE UNIVERSITY OF NEWCASTLE

1989

Published with the assistance of the Literature Board of the Australia
Council and the Hunter Water Board

First published in 1989
by the University of Newcastle, New South Wales, 2308,
Australia.

Printed in Australia by
Newcastle Camera Print,
106A Parry Street, Newcastle, 2300.

ISBN 0 7259 0663 4

Cover photograph by Allan Chawner

Arts for
Australians
**Australia** **Council**

# INTRODUCTION

Like painters, poets are fascinated by the eye. They often draw attention to the way the act of seeing changes what we see.

Many of the poets in this collection explore how what we see is changed by our perspective, by our position inside or outside the limits of the frame, and by the properties of the eye itself.

John Bennett's "Blackwattle Bay" does all this, while remaining anchored to the real water of a real bay. The judges of this year's Hunter Water Board/Mattara Poetry Prize were struck by its originality and unanimously awarded it the Prize in the Open section.

Martin Johnston's "In the Refectory of the Ognissanti" earned very high commendation. His poem provides an urbane account of our experience of reality as the painted boundary between art and life dissolves.

Throughout the collection motifs recur: painters, painting, paintings, and women reminiscent of those Rubens painted — Florence, and Europe as an artifact the poet is astonished to find him/herself actually walking through, touching its treasures. It was when I noted this that I decided to appropriate — almost — the title of Moussorgsky's piano suite.

In the Under Twenty-five section the winner chosen by the judges was Gabrielle Daviau, for "In Between the Going — I Came." The theme of her poem, "(I love)" opens up a rich other way of reading the anthology.

The observant will have seen that Allan Chawner's cover photograph loops and seems to join itself at the back. The match is close because of the apparent curving of space generated by the panning lens of Allan's beloved Widelux camera.

This collection is chosen from the entries to the 1989 Hunter Water Board/Mattara Poetry Prize — the ninth of its kind. My fellow judges were Judith Rodriguez and Michael Wilding. My sincere thanks to them for making the task both efficient and harmonious.

I owe a continuing debt of gratitude to the Hunter Water Board, who contributed the money for the Prize and much more, and to the Board's staff for their generous support and assistance throughout the year. I wish to mention the enthusiastic support of the newly retired Managing Director, Mr Allan McLachlan, Mr Glenn Turner, the Chairman of the Board, Mr Anthony G. Wright, the Acting Managing Director, and Ms Amanda Hainsworth. Without their assistance the Prize would not have existed.

I wish also to thank the Literature Board of the Australia Council for its continued support, the benefit of which is passed directly to the poets involved.

The University of Newcastle, the Vice-Chancellor, Professor Keith Morgan, and members of my own Department, Professor David Frost, Marie Hill and Wendy Pringle, have liberally given of time and resources, as has Brenda Twiss, who typed the text of the anthology. My friends and colleagues, especially Christopher Pollnitz, Mark Crowley and Keryl Kavanagh provided that support and help in time of need without which anthologists do not run.

Finally, to all the entrants to the Prize, my thanks for the privilege of reading their work.

*Paul Kavanagh*

# CONTENTS

ROBERT ADAMSON

from *WARDS OF THE STATE, AN ABSTRACT BALLAD*

"In my own land I am a foreigner;
Beside a hearth I shiver and ferment"
— Francois Villon

# THE OLD CHILDREN

They speak for themselves, though in a code
of unmaking, in slurred vowels, a burst
of laconic guttural that fends off action —
what's uttered between them could pass
for warning or affection; they rehearse
for nothing.  These are the Serapaxed mornings
of sun burning the blue calligraphy of skin
tattoos, here a beauty parlour works
the Alnite Coffee Bar's desolate laminex —
Though don't drop your guard just yet
with easy pity and exploit this new habitat
with condescending, there's no language
here for conscience, no visual concept —
this vernacular putters between voice-box
and burnt lungs: their poetry, drawn
with a spray-pack, describes a stark economy
and mocks the slick jargon of cash —
this anti-commerce has made its way from dank
board-rooms in stormwater drains, bypassed
the grim service of dole-queues, has sidled out
into the light without style, with nothing to say.

# Hot-Dogs & Alchemy

Shadow walks the wharf on a line of sun
through the silver air of Wooloomooloo

by the calm harbour, she holds a rose
in a bunch of crushed cellophane,

along by the drunks lined up like stumps
with brown paper wrapped around plonk

Shadow sits in the corner to cut and cook
a spoon of speed with a flame

from her flickering plastic Bic.
Don't picture the image of Christ's fish

spiked in dots on the back of her hand:
take this as a scene within a scene

Shadow's just turned seventeen today
she tries to dress like death

and succeeds, a black leather belt's slung
across her chest studded with skulls

the size of sparrow eggs, she has a way
with style as if every day's a carnival —

seagulls squabble between the marker buoys
and the hot-dog stand, a pack of mongrels bark

in the lane, O Meaning sweet Meaning
sings Shadow, will I still find you if I look.

# PETROL SNIFFING

A red shell on a yellow can: a joke
before experience — and all the money boxes

left in a corner, jagged open.
The children bumping soft foreheads

in morning steam; a prickly scent trickles
from a cap, hands too young to shake

tremble: the heavy metal fumes sink home.
We have tomorrows to eliminate,

though who knows how long the brain
can take the fingers of vapour

that soothe the brain — Any bad dream
dissolves to the touch of a rubber snake

that dribbles its menthol from cracked lips.
Give it names and call us sick

but your real drugs cost a sister's lunch,
and the whiskey's in your sin-bin;

Southern Comfort's for that lucky bunch
who can afford their own extinction

in style, oh sure it's a luxurious joke —
though you can't joke when you're flat broke;

it's a plastic bag when you're on the nod —
Don't think we can't see you getting off on misery.

# SONG

Over the top of a spiked fence a boy
carefully moves through barbed-wire,
years go before him as he escapes
the days he has lived through, nights
with storm smudged moons appear
in his dream of freedom, the wire tangles
and a day comes with his mother
walking away, he handles sharp loops
a metal-worker with an arc of molten ore
falling through air into the shape
he has made for his freedom, for him
freedom's fire and dances before
and behind, now his blood is free
in his hands, unfolding spikes in a fence
his thoughts are wings and he glides
from a shadow the shape of his father's voice,
over the wire, in space.

# SIGN THIS:

I will sign anything in case someone
notices, my name means nothing
in reality, no bank takes it seriously
and shops call for the police
at the sound of it, the police see it
written on reports and throw
them into the shredders; my son rubs
it from the envelope he uses
to carry his father's photograph in;
my name is shit so I won't plague
you with the details, I can't give it away
and it follows me through hell,
and when I was talking to my mother about
funerals and stuff I started to think
well, what are they going to put on my grave.

# CODA:

Who is saying what's between us?  Lives and words,
what have we got in common after all
pouring through art's funnel with you already full
of desolate sunsets over Mosman or Balmain —
What's between us other than the noise of language
I point to the bitterness of a man who
in the face of extinction, in a toxic harbour of sound
has stared carefully at a lonely moon drifting
across arteries of existence lapping heaven's shore.
I offer my family, my dead grandfather
what's heaven other than a poet's metaphor?
on the un-polluted sands of Dee Why Lagoon
where the act and its description meet
my father who dragged his lungs through the Homebush
brick-yard kilns for the endless rent —
so let me offer you a bitterness distilled
by blind drunk hoons in the pub's six o'clock swill —
my brothers mumbling their hearts away into football
scores, my mother turning away from the judge
at children's court while I watched my memories dance
out patterns on a fowl-house roof; though
here's the kind of narrowness you get in truth
from a man who's never told it.  I offer
this as half-learned magic picked up in the proof
of poetry along with all the fool's gold of a trance
induced by morning glory smothering the primrose —
Great-Works — and for you, whoever you are, sagging
branches of mulberries and the luxury of a grandmother
mottled with flour by the fuel-stove.

# JOHN BENNETT

# BLACKWATTLE BAY

## 13 FIBONACCI SONNETS

for Ian Bettinson

. . . further in by the oblique fishing fleet.  Next
I intercept some semaphore, a porthole sets a price
by light and calmly the bridge swings, boats leave.
Pelicans too have their own hunting grounds, coastal
outlandish and secret.  Signs warn of sharks alive.

The gods watch the spectacle.  Seagulls playfully
plucking white light in flight, illuminated shields
nosing slowly in triumphant procession; windscreens
of an army on the move track the sun, an example
of courage and apathy for naive poems.
In more explicit scenes, Homer would have powered
steel lasers to invent their victims, honest men
acting for life, smeared head to toe in pig's blood.

An art class on easels struggles to open up
a picture of perspectives, deserving a camera
natura, expecting mimesis before the real work
of marooning adjectives and packing up all
the other words into superstitious narratives.

Sunlight wells up on the glass world.  It allows
a bottle brush with gangling red flowers to be
cleansed by bubbles of slippery light
as it leans over the modulated surface smoothed
locally by the self-conscious spectra of oil.
How is everything put together, quartz-work
or quark-work, sutures invisible?
Is it all done with mirrors, or microscopes?

Under such favourable atmospheric conditions
clarity probes the shadow corners
of the soft offal-like brain,
just as a surgeon's sterile instrument cuts
and connects insistent visions and utopias.

Cell by cell imagination triggers the retina,
responding to a beauty on edge,
certain the plumage is blue and the electrical/
chemical configurations "true."
Highlights coruscate a bee's eye in clover
flowing from flower to opulent flower,
returning to the hive to dance;
pollination by chance nourishing the poem.

Lining Victoria Road on slippery slopes of fantasy
the advertisements are as aware of the golden mean
as Dürer or say Seurat.  The scene is set inside
a cibachrome B of vain blue air and water, capable
of subsuming everything to tone and composition.

Absorbed into the eye, everything
becomes an element, assuming equivalence
as in a landscape photograph.  Everything
in the picture demands attention.
The frame clings to thirteen lines.
Each line a branch that creaks like wood
and like wood stretches beneath a sky
of memorable arboreal blueness.

An eye's mayhem, the organ of desire we use to do
now tends to stimulate and excite without
involving understanding.  Her face shines, sweats.
The rowing boat, dragonfly lean and light
takes for granted its hot slender motion.

There's no bleeding, the colours are discrete,
their patterns seamless; no space between the light
in the lattice because it's only light we see.
The atoms imagined in the furniture fill out our
molten flesh, sensate of interstellar distances
between each word.  The breeze tugs eagerly at
the page the pen dances on, searching out form
through a valence, a code or skeletal equation.

The fovea — is the open mouth,
the optical pathway of direct light,
"the best vision is from directly looking."
It's the only field free from blood-vessels
or nerve fibres in an inside out retina.

A fact used to counter an 18th century argument
from design: humans are more ingeniously made
than watches and so must have been designed by
a superior creator. Update: a watch is understood
by its purpose to tell, life deserves this analogy.
Proof belongs to booze not this shattering light
or an ontological argument, I watch instead
a beer bottle's compulsive bobbing, current caught.

The city floats so seriously, up to its neck
in solid grey conversation, its spires sunk
beneath a prospect of parapets, each one
a prestigious development.  Glass blooms
a fisherman's tale of billions of scarlet suns.

Why is abandoned to teleologia, to the form
work of planning permission, concrete secrets and
accountants' compulsive labours to avoid tax —
the landscape is carried off by the winners.
A pragmatic pelican, arms beating solidly
flying along the foreshore loop, passes feet away
and excretes a spiralling cohesion,
a silky white silhouette                a fish jumps.

Thoreau listens, sense accepting brutal facts like
the acoustics of wagtails dancing tree to tree or a
ship's siren of raw iron pressed to chest and belly,
not trying to look behind the light for the divine
as though mystery was earmarked for the sacred.

Looking for nothing in particular; there's no sign,
nothing unusual in the bay, God is invisible; just
enjoying the continuity no pause for breath or any
gathering of thought, swimming through the bright-
ness as the bees' droning converges on the traffic
moving smoothly once more past wavelets pecking on
the warm sandstone tongue I'm sitting on.  In a kind
of reverie, a token losing of a self for a while.

A grass blade as tall as centrepoint is pared to
prismatic beads, an entertainment from eyelash
fragmentation counting the drops of light.
Addition naturally progresses to fibonacci numbers
whose "properties appear to be inexhaustible."

Not  wanting to make too much of all this or
the  shadows tucked under the gulls' wings or
the  cat flopped against my back and purring or
the  dog snapping up seagulls into the air, or
the  kingfisher's startling presence on
the  barbed wire perimeter of the old house on
the  point, rumoured to become a writer's centre;
but  disappointment is not a recent phenomenon.

Galileo suggested that mathematics holds the key
to understanding the universe.  I can't count
seven colours in a rainbow though Newton used
that number thinking it sacred (but not fibonacci).
His beautiful world is displaced to one we live in.

Disturbed by the sight of men bopping on the moon,
extras grudgingly fucking, blood vessels threshing,
the agony of living incremental in a zebra's moving
decay (a horse or cow disguised in striped skin),
the apple shot or a painting sublime & sacramental —
I write.  Wary of commodities & creations that grow
by themselves, seducing our interest, reducing it
to paintings (or painters) not painting.

I write, and quote Tom Rayworth, "Writing becomes
the only thing that is not petroleum by-product,
or a neat capsule available without prescription."
You and I both work, overlay, imagine, and correct
audience and critic to the metamorphic process.

Art for Gadamer derives from play
both are subject to themselves, existing
only as experienced.  Huizinga surmised that play
created culture but is now deteriorating into
false play entertaining agendas essentially human.
Dewey saw life as drama, participation, integral
to good and beauty (the Greeks used the one word)
to which Keats added truth in the service of Art.

In compensation for God leaving meanings behind,
for the failure of natural theology, Ruskin's
response to beauty was with his whole being.
The airwaves bristle with talk of theoria
and nostalgic whinges on art's decline to pleasure.

"I love this thing that from his background he
 transcended everything.  He's a painterly painter
 a one off, he'd get up at dawn to see whatever
 but took it further.  It was all about painting,
 what landscape is.  Turner painted what he felt.
 He was one of the greatest perspective artists;
 a mark would read perfectly as a cow on a wash on
 some paper, he didn't have to put the details in."

Resplendent light is caught tangled
in the junk and jetsam, torn plastic
waves like ocean kelp or lethargic cilia
bullied by an inconsequential incoming tide.
A pied cormorant is counted up at twenty-five.

In some stray history two solitary fishermen,
one a woman, sit on the fringe of the world
touching thin threads taut with a silver light.
They take the strain of the steep metallic skin
and wait for the weekend to bite.
A fire burns on a balcony, laughter overbalances,
glasses chink and drain the last drops
of colour from the water views . . .

JAVANT BIARUJIA

from *JAVA*

# PASURUAN

Lawalawalawalawang!
Paspaspaspasuruan!
Malamalamalamalang!
the bus pulls to a jerky halt for the conductor to haul in
either thru the side or back door villagers otherwise
standing by the roadside he — not much more than a boy
— hangs from the back door singing his litany of
placenames

Lawalawalawalawang!

at Pasuruan women with towel cushioned basins on their
heads pass by the windows inveigling us to buy peanuts
soya bean cakes fruit or cigarettes boys come in with ices
tea bottled drinks a man parcels out folded newspapers
onto our laps reciting the headlines a beggar's hand
reaches in thru a window for alms

Faris rests his hand on mine don't unfold the paper
unless you wish to buy it soon everybody is handing
back their papers unopened but far from disheartened the
villager with teeth stained from betelnut cracks a joke at
which everyone laughs

JOHN BRAY

# VISITATION

### after the Homeric Hymn

Impatient with the goddesses' reproaching
For intermittent earthly sexual poaching
In animal, divine or human shapes,
Enjoying stray amours and quasi-rapes,
The gods petitioned Zeus somehow to plan
To implicate a goddess with a man.
He grants the prayer.  But who shall be selected?
The two fierce virgins are at once rejected,
Athena wrapped in warfare and technology,
Artemis testing patents in toxology.
Pleasing to catch Hera succumbed to siege:
But then she is his wife.  Noblesse oblige.
"No, Cyprian Aphrodite set the trap
To our confusion.  Let her take the rap."
Accordingly into her view he flings
The young Anchises by Mount Ida's springs,
Watering his cattle, bending to unfold
His trim-set buttocks faintly brushed with gold,
His sturdy thighs — enough.  Fired by these sights
From her own fuel the goddess self-ignites,
Seized with a furious itch to intermesh
Immortal limbs with fleeting mortal flesh.
  In Cyprus she is rubbed, anointed, bathed,
Perfumed, bejewelled, in flaming silks enswathed,
With half success endeavouring to abate
The customary splendours of her state.
Nature is not deceived.  Behind her tread
The roses spring and bloom in white and red.
The birds are making love on every bough,
The ram seeks out the ewe, the bull the cow,
And leopards copulate around the track

That leads uphill towards Anchises' shack.
Aroused by these phenomena he sees
Her come, refulgent, gliding through the trees.
"Goddess!" he says, and sinks upon his knees.
Dimming, she speaks. "Goddess! I'm no such thing.
I am the daughter of a Phrygian king.
Your reputation's fame has spread so wide
Hermes has brought me here to be your bride.
If you agree, at once we make dispatch
And here and now we consummate the match."
"A likely tale," Anchises must have thought.
Perilous the gifts the Fates bestow unsought.
But youthful pride and rising virile lust
Shred his prudential scruples into dust.
"Gladly," he says, "I take you for my bride."
He picks her up and carries her inside.
He sets her down and pulls off brooches, rings,
Bracelets and necklaces in spiral strings,
And while she stands demure with downcast eyes
Strips off the clinging silk, unbares her thighs,
And lifts her up, his palliasse to share,
Spread with the skins of wolf and lion and bear.
They consummate the cross-specific deed.
The immortal womb is charged with mortal seed.
  The gods need little slumber. She resumes
Her splendid emblems, towers in height, relumes.
"Trojan," she says, "Why do you sleep so long?
Your first remark to me was not far wrong.
I had a fancy for a mortal lover."
"Cypris!" he says and sinks beneath the cover.
"What happens next? Am I to be struck dead,
Or on a wheel of fire for ever sped,
Or with immortal life but senile age
Shrink to a fading beep inside a cage?"
"None of these things," she said, "If you are wise.
Nine months will see our son materialize,
Then trusted to the mountain nymphs to rear,
Instructed, when he's five, to bring him here.
Cherish him well. I shall watch from above

With interest, and a mother's distant love.
Only be sure to keep concealed my part,
Or fear to feel the thrust of Heaven's dart."
But who is always tongue-clogged when he sups?
He boasts about his conquest in his cups.

## GABRIELLE DAVIAU

# IN BETWEEN THE GOING — I CAME

In reach now, that piece of river always with new waters
and I'll be calm to sidewalk, repeat and reply myself
again more shrugged inside Japara dog foraying under
blackberries, repeated, rebrambled sustained in past
(N.B. "a foreign country remarked by Hartley")
Where crouched, your Lee Coopers stretched to the point
of my return: clasping dog, scuffed, nuggetless snapped laces
(I love) bent and tortured comfortably brown boots, the torn,
ragged back pocket barely seen over water
Sun maggotting the three brass eyelets of your boots (I love)
my dog my man my river myself
my coming my return my love my madness
never framed but glass undered, you, you there water running
at back stark leaf blown away trees I leaf through
grassed jean knees, your pages and tight seams your elbowless
unholy jumpers (I love) with bristled face stubbled and laughing
eyes (momentarily) masking tension, frustration, I antagonise
and antagonise, not liking this part of myself yourself his self
her selfed, chafed lovishness  come at man
ourselves karma  atman  oneself
photo you, dog, river the go-between for my going my leaving
my loving, no nightshades — willows claw the banks and there is
     . . . sun.
black belladonna berries your eyes  and I knew him (sic) . . . Bible
sic . . . the dog ignores and pushing and pulling this closeness
— spoonfed — perhaps spooning was all we had  drown me in holey
jumpers (I love)

I am flying back on gossamer wings to your nest
to my river my dog my man  in my/our love my obsession
bereft and atropined  layed on grassy verge next river
with camera over heart reincarnating all the photos I've loved

SARAH DAY

# THE FISH-FEEDERS

Darwin

They have exhausted the museums, galleries, bars,
turned down the last road to the steps on the edge of the ocean.
This is the end of the tourist run.

They come like ancient Greeks to the oracle
and the fish, flesh to flesh, clear-eyed, old-bottle green,
swim the miraculous response at their feet.

In the aqua nudge, pummel of opaque flesh
they are sensuous as sumos, yet bloodless —
spontaneous creations of water.

Harbingers, these great fish are prophetic,
healers, moralists, teachers, they come
in a plash of white fin and swallow-tail at high tide

to eat bread.  In the pitch of each pupil's dim disc
eons are suspended, the whole reflected future
in glassy lens of huge unblinking eye.

Their race is infinity's loop.  The nets are full,
the fish-feeders take plenty and leave untouched.
This older than ancient rite is like being born again.

# DIANE FAHEY

## from LISTENING TO A FAR SEA

# GLAUCUS, SON OF MINOS

His young son is lost —
Minos orders the seer
to find him.

The cellar flickers
round his candle:
the seer contemplates,

as they close,
an owl's eyes,
ochre and tawny,

points to
the jar brimming
with honey.

A gold serpent
coils and
re-enters the jar,

as the body
is raised aloft,
into a circle

of lamps, faces . . .
"Give him life,"
orders the king;

and, when he breathes,
"Teach him your
secrets —

stay here while he grows."
When, at last,
the seer may leave,

he has Glaucus spit
in his mouth — frees him
from so much wisdom:

too much for
that small frame
to carry.

An image of coiling
light, is all
the boy retains —

light, gold and
sinewy, connecting him
to that sweet, curved darkness.

STEPHEN GILFEDDER

# THE MUNITIONS DIVERS

for Joseph Gilfedder
killed in action
May 31, 1916

Three blasts from the whistle
starts a crazy dance
of wheelchairs spinning
in the summer heat.
On leave from their nursing homes
the two surviving widows, ninety-odd,
are anchored by their bags of duty free.
(Why shouldn't old women
have Givenchy and Johnnie Walker Black?)
They manoeuvre the wreath
from reluctant relatives
over the sliprail
onto the shifting, oily sea.
The ferry circles once
and heads from the Jutland Bank,
riding the current back to Hartsholm.

Beneath a sky like white-out
the North Sea curls
and breaks its tremulous green
among the tufted hillocks
and the twisted bracken
where thick-necked horses
are turned to pasture.
When we dock clutching each other
spray from the surging undertow
is splashed across our faces
like holy water
as the ship's bell rings.

The buoys of the lobster pots
dribbling tears of rust
pitch and swell in line.
All night from the guesthouse
we hear the yawning cast of the anchor chains
pulling at the changing tide.
Restless at the window
I see you bobbing white
against the phosphorescent sea.

Old Mr Olsen who holds the keys
of the Municipal Museum
opens the unfrequented schoolhouse
on the quay as promised on the sign outside
"By appointment, Tuesdays and Fridays only."
He stands like an exhibit in the half-light
among the display cases of the past.
He spreads his hands.
All thanks to the co-operative he says.
From an English transcript stapled to the handbook
he recites that the coast was famous for its wrecks.
The locals gathered everything washed ashore:
the sea-turned wood became an architrave,
exotic fruits were soaked in akvavit,
a crate of best burgundy
was hoarded for Midsummer Night.
Cottages were ornamented with the wrack
and families photographed with their trophies —
a horn of ivory, a Parisian mode.
Coconut husks were painted
and lined the window sills.
From winter to winter the dead grey sea
rolled back to leave among the harvest
the unknown sailors buried on the headland.

"Here I am as a baby with my parents."
Mr Olsen points at the black-clothed figures

standing on the causeway at low tide.
"Behind us you see the shapes
of the sailors from the great battle.
The village worked for weeks to bury them."
Out in the sunlight
we climb the hill and inspect
the rows of regulation graves,
German and British lying together.
Along the cliff top
the Scandanivian nudists stand
in Walkmans and sunglasses
watching the arrival of the dive launch
with its catch of copper cable
and brass shell casings.
All week the dull tremor
of detonations out to sea
has resonated the Heineken sign
outside the hotel bar,
a shimmering wind song for the dead.

Rolling his wet-suit to his waist
Irish Dave taps out his pipe
against the wire cage of salvage.
Sponging encrusted salt
from the lycra he spreads
an Admiralty map
and pinpoints boilers, funnels, twelve inchers,
the shattered hulls with their invisible crews,
spread along the narrow channel.
The reclaimed metal ashtray souvenirs remain unsold.
His rolex fires tracers in the sun.
He speaks of waking in the night
believing he has drowned,
the off-season on the Reef,
siren brown women,
and the cathedrals of coral
where a man can lose himself.

# JOCKEYS AT ST KILDA PIER

They float
like ghosts of children
in the hot sea bath
the Sunday after the races.
Thin white arms
flap ineffectually against the steam
and transparent faces
turn to the stranger
for affirmation of their denial.
Today they will barely eat or drink.
Yet those delicate wrists
have the power to make or break
larger men and their happiness.
A few have perfected
smoking on their backs,
cigarettes held above the water,
beacons in the sulphurous gloom.
The sinewy bodies nose and bump,
each tragically mirrored
to twice its size.
Earlier they could have been mistaken
for dancers in their Italian shoes,
prancing onto the pier
from imported limousines.
Rubbing down, the retired hoop
slaps red whip marks
on the skinny frames
and with a final drum roll
sends them to the sauna.
Their wish is to become still smaller.

# LAYING THE CAT'S EYES

At a distance backed up we hear
the dull stamp
of the feeder.
Then the roadman swivels
his sign to go
and only then we see
the task at hand.
Two reflectors equidistant
laid perfectly in rows
twenty metres apart.
It requires an elemental skill:
we are talking about an exact
twenty metres repeated
to get that nighttime filigree
running through the dark.
Passing the crew at speed
we salute our thanks.
They do not look up.
For every one of us
there's another stretch of road
and targets to be reached.
We are measured simply
in bins of sparkling jewels.
Picnicking miles away we hear
the lumbering engine
catching up
planting its sightless eyes.

ALAN GOULD

# TREELOPPERS

Always before you are quite ready —
you're in the shower or on the phone —
before the suburb's cool vestibules
of birdsong, and your lawn, prismatic
with sprinkler-dew, can be got ready
for the shattering onset of their solos,

they arrive in a ute with muffler-rattle,
and the boom-boom of fifties rock;
"Horizon Modifiers Unlimited"
is emblazoned on the bonnet, and
you note a sticker on the tailgate
that urges "Eat more koalas."

They accept the tea, black with several,
and begin the daylong crossfire of banter;
the blonde swaggery one who hulks
around the cigarette he's making
tells you they're gunna drop the tree
in one shabang right there between

the greenhouse and the Audi, no need
to move the pot-plants.  But even as
it dawns on you the wisecracks are
a means of subtle surveillance, he's turned
to Naccers, his gaunt offsider, who,
you gather, tree-lops to finance his calling

for translating Arabic poetry, and,
returning his tobacco, says, "Nah,
leave it all to ol' Fumble and Grumble."
Once it is established they're here

as much for the job as loose subversion
of both your world and theirs, they start,

with spanners, oil, conferrals, till one
with animal sudden-ness, leaps at a branch
and shins skyward with a rope.
Whatever your plans for today, forget them
in favour of this craning theatre,
this lofty, improvising ballet

on a stringy, disappearing stage.
Remark how utterly a chainsaw
takes possession of a day
with its not quite monotonal plainsong —
its bursts of unbridled hype, its low
growls of impatience — how it reveals

shortlived beauties, say, the clay-red
roundels of an ironbark's cross-section,
or a lightning-white torso
cleft into dozens of lovely shoulders.
Theirs, the biggest on the market,
is nicknamed der Führer, with reason,

as its edged, unyielding tongue takes
the lead through layers of intransigence
with a snarl of pure aggression and
a furious spitting of dross. It is tackling
a blue gum gangrenous with bracket
fungus, and leaves your lawn, alas,

littered with blue-green plumage, as though
it were the killing-ground of a grand
pheasant shoot. Remark also,
how, for all their talk, their work
is founded on obedience to
a tree's intricate system of fulcrums,

how scarf-cut and back-cut abet
the tendencies of limb and trunk,
and how the dancer is watching for skew
or the rogue inward swing of a branch
as his mate lowers it on a rope
that uses the tree-barrel as a capstan.

It's this might prove the telling subversion,
this longing that wells like a sob, to be
alert to the immediacy of things,
to recover presence *there,* at the nexus
of animate balance and technical nous.
In their time, which is expensive,

they'll finish up and drive away
their ute hugely ruffed with foliage,
leaving your horizon modified.
You, and your house, of course, have been
representative, though personally
you've done quite well; you paid in cash,

refrained from fussing over details,
and suppressed the niggling feeling that
somehow you spent the day on trial.

# HIGH CLOUD CONVERSATION

A cirro-cumulus morning; the high chenille
comes drifting in from Burrinjuck and Yass,
slow as glass above the strawy flare of terrain.

Already the city is too far gone in employment,
too deep beneath its traffic râle, to catch
the mood the weather brings, allegro, expectant.

It is a day for loose employments, for making
rapid disco-light on cycle-paths,
where rosellas in their romany shawls dart-skip

among the poplars, where the wattles shimmer
in their froth of verdigris.  We'll tour
the aroma-zones, warm enclaves of eucalypt

federal with cantons of mown hay, with, here,
a seam of bitumen, here, a redolence of pine.
And an instant will hold, and then release,

a small cross boy slashing at a bush
with his stick, or two round women
throwing back their heads in the one laugh;

shall we go?  Or loaf, unguilty, in hammocks,
the morning lost to itself, our novels dropped
in favour of what the artless day might bring,

remarking in observant reverie how the wind
with its palette of whites invisibly crafts
that slow upper weather?  I might be saying,

(echoing some recent discontent,)
how the wind does so much more than merely
bother the air, as it purls and flattens and teases,

as it *elaborates*; elaborations that will not melt
entirely back into the language; we can, we do,
disclose the tricky ground that reconciles

what exists with the way in which it's known.
You, meanwhile, gazing at the high prairies,
those far Saskatchewans of snowy ploughland,

might answer as though from a conversation
yet to take place; *Yes, there is a time*
*or cast of mind perhaps, resembling closely*

*these cirrus mornings — not unhappy,*
*it is one's life adrift in a slow direction;*
*the overview as intricate as ever,*

*but somehow, what . . . ? too level? too detached?*
*too distant from the salient.* Maybe
to know this is also part of a life's work,

this easy taking in of leisurely floes,
too high, too slow to bother with horizons.

## MARTIN JOHNSTON

# IN THE REFECTORY OF THE OGNISSANTI

In the refectory of the Ognissanti
at four in the echoing afternoon
lunch has been left in front of the Last Supper:
three almost empty mineral-water bottles,
breadcrumbs, plastic cups on the trestle table
that seems set up to echo Ghirlandaio's.
You could pass a drink to Judas.
Birds fly out of tromp l'œil into yesterday's loggia
where Peter's half-raised knife cuts sandwiches.
It's like the recurring "j"
you change into "i" when you're editing German,
like the way there's no way
to see the Gattamelata except on TV.
One experience always deflects another,
a billiards of aborted possibilities,
and what you see you've brought with you like a picnic.
You walked into the shaft of light
in the painted background where all the lines met
and it rained uniquely and all day on the poplars,
the burnt-umber castles, the straciatella ice-cream.
The roadside was littered with porcupine quills
like tramps' signs or Ogham.  You're a poet,
she said before going, well, here's a quill.
In the refectory of the Ognissanti
you hear in a corner the familiar scuttle
of a theory of aesthetics going to ground.
The fox in the vineyard, the roebuck in the mist
were bright singularities without a syntax,
the distant hills just beyond the window
a russet and green infolding, dimensionless and precise,
and over Pienza a faded rainbow
embodies the idea of destination,
but there's a wall behind the birds.

Now the green grapes are gone, and the speed of fresco
pulls haloes oblate, moons two days off full,
and among more stars than you thought possible
something untimely howling in the woods
that bristle down to the river's edge suggests
alternative skylines best left unpainted. Later,
there's less of the lunch left, though you're still alone.
You thought you'd flattened Ghirlandaio:
you thought a pale blue beehive mattered more.
You try to make your provenance impeccable.
The ancient codices speak of a white tower
floating in silver clouds on the horizon
a tapestry of insinuating hills. There are directions
for painting blue-green lizards among the blackberries,
an orange three-legged dog breaststroking through long grass,
directions for editing and reattribution.
In the refectory of the Ognissanti
you taste the thin flavour of actuality
you carry around like an abridged Vasari.
Rainwater sinks in and hollows behind your eyes
a workshop where the restorers wash off varnish
and critics scoff at the flat vivid wall
you walk back into, licking melted ice-cream.
Offering up your void, you invent perspective,
the birds fly out of the wall,
perch on the turrets of the unattainable tower
and peck outrageous signatures
on dissolving frescoes you authenticate.
The landscape folds neatly into your head
which you carry carefully as rare majolica
out into the rain that sweeps the Arno,
making sure that nothing rattles.
And very carefully, not stepping on the lines,
you tiptoe like Uccello
in a fevered abstraction on vanishing points,
green slate of the river washed in gunmetal grey,
having your cake and eating it,
from the refectory of the Ognissanti.

JILL JONES

from *AS A CITY WAKES SO IT DREAMS*

"... new buildings, scaffolding, blocks,
old suburbs, turn into allegory,
and memories are heavier than stone."
— *Le Cygne*, Charles Baudelaire

# A CONSTRUCTION OF RADIANCE

The world recedes and reveals the world —
what one artist sees, out of times of turbulence —
one artist's revolution.
Now on dark brown walls, reverentially lit,
briefly,
for our appreciation.

Like tourists at the Quay we watched the harbour,
then turned our backs and walked,
past old stone walls, the new glass towers,
walked to the Gallery just to see
the exhibition, *Turner Abroad,*
framed flat planes, three-dimensioned by their own light,
labelled with times of upheaval.
Is this what the artist sees — painting in dangerous times
between revolutions, 1789, 1848, and the wars —
a continent lit by a different sun and a light within,
as though this was the revolution,
the overturning of the grey sky
and the green and pleasant land?
Forever now the Italian campagna is being born
from a yellow sun,
a road in Switzerland leads to a radiant mountain,
he called it *Bellinzona from the Road to Locarno,*
walls, towns and people under the colour filter slowly

to the eye through pigment and water,
ghosts within the reality,
and a mountain pass, *The Pass of Faido*, swirls
out of Turner's imagination, coming
from deep within the flat paper, emerging like
the changes of the century,
and the artist's vision, the artist's death, in 1871.

But we return again to the harbour
with our art catalogue, late afternoon light
does not obscure the scaffolding at the Quay,
the graffiti, official and unofficial,
proclaiming the hope of reconstruction,
signifying dust and garbage and money.
We sit by the waste bins, plastered
with anti-litter signs, lying felled, dented and rusting,
dribbling newspapers and tomato sauce over the brown grass,
and seagulls screech and dip and scavenge.

The radiant mountain fades in the catalogue (plate 111),
but we ignore the other mountains of refuse,
as the night quickens,
allowing the myth of the harbour to emerge,
and the unknown busker, fading in the dusk,
the piper at the Quay, skirls
and silences even the scavengers,
and
          the world recedes and
                    reveals the world,
again.

# THE STRANGER'S KISS

I dream sometimes of becoming anonymous, alone,
then connecting with some eyes,
which widen a second, then cut, turn away,
for me, acknowledgement, the stranger's kiss.
Or half an hour over coffee, solitary,
but two tables away,
you mime for yourself and the other,
even better if there are mirrors
along the walls and you can pretend
to read or write or contemplate distance.
In the eighteen months I have sat here,
on and off through jobs and seasons,
I have even nodded, once spoken of weather,
stretched out brief encounters.

# OUR CONSPIRACY

October rain makes the footpath slippery
but in raincoats, disguised, we step up from the street.
You smile, you turn to me
but I'm remembering another life.
We sit down in the cafe like anyone else —
lovers in a dangerous world — (it's spring, of course).
I turn out my pockets at the table
looking for clues, you pick up the menu, stare
at the window, October rain, Sydney shines . . .

Like artists, like scientists entranced, we look around,
touching under the table, in front of us the indications:
bus tickets, dollar coins, cards made from plastic,
telephone numbers on scraps of paper.
I sort through the means of exchange,
you glance through the menu, acknowledging danger,
and pleasure, ignoring the espresso hiss,
the headlines of my newspaper, and the last thirty years —
death in the family, the death of god . . .
and regeneration — out there in spring rain,
in here, rush of fresh caffeine,
between your lips and mine, speaking about weather,
our barometers, warmth and moisture,
signs of our complicity.

Look at you look at me look at you,
behind disguises, almost,
like undercover agents, conspirators behind mirrors,
mirrors behind us and window glass reflects our forms,
the wet city gleams in, I see danger everywhere,
out there, the city gets wetter and wetter,
and the heat is coming, you are more careful,
checking the bill, then we move together, pulling out
money, grabbing our raincoats, anticipating
the footpath still slippery . . .

PETER KIRKPATRICK

# THE WALK AROUND THE LAKE

Lake Wendouree, Ballarat, Victoria

for Peter and John

Begin with the transcendental and you'll end
in relationships: discussion is a circle
walked around the water of an idea
that curves upon the limitations of saying
world inside of world outside of world.

Joggers pass, re-pass, running their mystic circuits
while we remain pedestrian, prosaic and passive,
stopping for a piss, to ride the swings,
or to be hissed at by protective swans
shepherding their cygnets with hooked necks.

Plato, Heidegger and Nietzsche blend imperceptibly
into stories of the Jewish ex-wife's family
who argued endlessly and made no sense
except to one another,
and accounts of a lost academic domestic life in Washington,
and of the late morning dream of holding a Rubens woman.
The Word, it seems, irretrievably is flesh.

If there's an argument that ends in *light*,
maybe it's not a destination
but a continual beginning
as everyday as dawn, warm beds and daily papers;
a story that always gets retold, re-edited,
to wind up as the stuff of opera — Wagnerian or soap —
even while the breakfast cup is drunk,
the car is started, the train is boarded,

and the shapeless afternoon takes on a body
(your own).

Ideas bend into the meniscus of things,
into the shifting dialectic of ourselves
against the lake's peeled lead,
against a golden wind blowing with the intermittent sun.
From where we talk our feet turn
serenely with the undulating ring of the horizon,
set in the east with Warrenheip and Buninyong,
those mountain stones almost as big as words
— ruins of a former proof concerning matter.

But it's with cloud mass after cloud mass
that the afternoon spins on.  Us with it.
Recycled joggers grimace: vague recognition, maybe.
They fret about, make sacrifices for the physical;
it's obvious our bodies are neglected kids.
In evidence of which our circle leaks
into the tail of a Q and trickles
towards the all important question, *ice cream*?
Great minds think alike.

Just as fools seldom differ.
Returning, the white sunlit room waits like a filmset
for three lonely actors to wonderfully enter.
Only the nude looking out of the window
and holding a steaming teacup is missing.

# NORA KROUK

"The old man is empty for the holiday of her body . . ."
— John Millett

Holiday is all done:
percolating spiced juices
ripe apples and plums
pulsing elastic flesh
tight skin.

Colours are fading now:
blue is blue not quite blue
and the aromas — yes, yes,
floral and fresh cut grasses
pierce, but where's the brass?
Gongs  bells ringing
medley of scents and sounds
undertow of sharp musk?
Blood  honeyed and heavy
blood  singing and light
and the bright dome
offering world's wonders
to the holiday of her body?


Gone.    Done.

Things  now exist
in their own context.
She savours words.

# VOICES

*Lily.*

Lily returned to the room. Mama was gone now. Stuffed into a Black Maria speeding this very minute into the unknown . . .

M A M O C H K A! Mama, who only last night hugged her and wept for Papa. Gone.

In the room Lily staggered to her corner. The pallet they'd shared with Mama has been made that morning: two lumpy pillows and a faded quilt over patched, grey sheets. One of the pillows was missing.

She could hear the landlady in her corner cursing the enemies of the people.

*Geta.*

Part of her mind shrank to a frozen dot: corridors, guards'
footfalls, keys turned on the outside.

The other part sent out flares, burst into hysterical laughter: — a
spy? Who, me? Heh! I'm not quite seventeen . . . Papa's
favourite girl . . . This is some kind of joke . . . a
misunderstanding . . .

Let me go home!

Home?

Once in the yard they fouled up the time-table. She saw some
male prisoners shuffle out and, suddenly: Papa's voice:
DOCHENKA! DOCHKA! Her Papa's voice.

Once. For the rest of her life.

*Geta.*

Mornings the mist was bad and some of us dazed. I don't
know . . . a rotten night maybe . . . something.

They shouted: — keep in the column or I'll shoot!

They were only kids. Often straight from their kholhoz. Just
kids, you know, frightened . . . as guards responsible for every
prisoner.

As though anyone could even attempt to escape from a marching
column.

Olga stumbled and fell out of line. The guard panicked and
pulled the trigger. Olga was on the ground . . . We kept walking.

Yes, somebody picked her up. Shot in the stomach. She died
that night.

The boy only did it because he was scared. A peasant boy, at
five in the morning, guarding the State's enemies . . . with a gun.
Just a kid.

*Yefim.*

Life in Shanghai, for him, was late hours at work, chess, wenching. Life was falling in love and marriage. Delayed fatherhood.

He did not know what happened to them. Just   something. There was no word. And no one to ask.

They had gone back (back in the thirties) prompted by motives as simple as loss of work in Harbin and failure to contact a relative in America.

They had gone back, but he, an only son, stayed on in China: inexplicably, there was a hitch with his visa.

The news from Russia seeped like a blood stain. General news. No word from his family.

News of arrests and trials. His fear made the connection. But, no . . . it couldn't be! Couldn't? Or . . . Why?

When the word came it was from his kid sister, hurriedly scribbled, without return address:
— Papa is very ill . . . and sister . . . Mama is now recovering. Sends her love.

. . . Life was success, increasing comforts, a sense of self-worth . . . perforated by ulcers. Unshed tears gathered inside his chest . . . acid drip eating away stomach lining.

Over the years there were sporadic letters from sister Lily, now signed by her married surname with a return address.

She'd named a son after their Father. Now he knew that Papa was dead.

*Eva.*

He grieved in an insular, private way.  Slept badly.

I married him knowing little about his people.  They had gone back.  Their fate was unknown.

There was a shadow   and hints that things were wrong.

Years later we had a letter.  Later still a message of harsh despair:
— Urgently send painkillers.  Mama in great pain.

We managed to forward some medicine through diplomatic channels.  It was too late.

Facts we could only guess at, made for a vague picture: arrests, long sentences.  Papa's death in a camp.

A manufactured scenario lacked detail: knocks on the door . . . the Black Marias . . .

My husband guarded his nightmares.

Twenty years on, in Israel, an immigrant cousin from Russia said to me, matter-of-factly: — His Father was shot.  Didn't you know?

I cried: — No, no, don't bring it up!  For Heaven's sake, don't tell him!

But migrants from Russia have their own code.

At dinner, serving us blintzes and jam, she watched my husband . . . mused — Now, when did our cousin Anya write last?  Let's see . . . it was the year your Father was shot.

My husband remained still.  No questions.  Later — no tears.

His ulcers are the size of fifty cent pieces.  Small change.

*Geta.*

She said: — They never beat Mama or me.  They never touched us.  Never.

Her face was working, but her eyes, nearly blind now behind thick lenses, were    fixed.

She said: — They did their job.  They knew it was just an absurd script, but they had to . . .

I tried to ask questions.  Prying?  Yes, I suppose.

I asked: — Did they punish you?  For anything?  How did they . . . ?

Suddenly, she said: — Once, I was put in a box.  A closet.  A shallow closet.  Locked up in it — standing — for 36 hours.

She just came out with it.  Herself.  We wanted to know: how . . . how?  She  wouldn't  answer  then.

Later: — Your legs want to burst.

Later still: — I couldn't go on unless I turned that page.

*Geta.*

She speaks of the camp as of her youth. Of course that was the time.

She says: — Pyotr Semenich, our doctor, liked me a lot. He mentioned to a few friends that I had the most beautiful breasts he'd ever seen. Like a Rubens painting, he used to say . . . The word got to Alexei and he wanted to meet me.

Alexei was terribly thin, but a great womanizer. There were quite a few women, you know. Well, he managed it . . . that's how I got Bella, my first born.

Geta's face gets softer and younger. We have a chuckle about emaciated Alexei panting after her breasts.

— He was quite vain then about his conquests. And girls were surprised when he stuck by me. What have you got there, they asked, bells maybe? Yeah . . . I amused him all right.

Geta pulls gently at the skin tight dress over her 80 kg bulk. She likes these dresses and values firm flesh.

— He never told me about his past. I used to ask him often, but he wouldn't answer . . . Like he was born there: too thin, too fond of women and grog.

Afterwards, much later, when we were both out and married he offered to tell me about himself. It was too late. I told him I wasn't interested.

Our girls know nothing about their Father's beginnings. Only about his end.

*Geta.*

She comes for a visit and she is ready. Ready to face a strange world. Ready to let her family melt the barrier between a lost childhood and a life lost in an enactment of a kafkaesque hoax.

She comes to Sydney to interact. First time in the West after 50 years! She comes to forgive. She comes to shop.

Children and grandchildren are the fabric of life. Marriages, infidelities, pregnancies and abortions . . . The layer cake Mama baked in their childhood.

Her brother prepares albums to share with her their past life. Albums full of strange people, smiling, drinking and talking in various situations. Women in silks and furs. Flowers and exhibitions.

She cannot look. She tells them her eyes hurt. She thinks:
— Which year was that? When Mama and I . . . ? She hurts in a way that is not familiar. Lives, now touching, cannot mesh.

Her brother wants to talk about the Perestroika.

— Yes, yes, she says, Glasnost and all that shit.

— *Today* — yes!

Her brother uses many important words:
— A people's collective conscience. The irreversible change . . .

She says: — I really prefer sweet fruit. Bananas, when you can get them . . .

Her sister-in-law takes them to shops. And in an avalanche of jeans (for the boys), jumpers (for daughters), slithering silky (skin tight) jerseys, leather trimmed jackets and shoes and bags she loses herself, finds her lost youth, regains a foothold in slipping reality: all this has to fit into suitcases.

— Glasnost, says her brother. The papers today . . .

She is too busy. Grace Bros. in Chatswood is starting a sale.

MARTIN LANGFORD

# CLAPPING

I clap.

It is better than silence.

Hands cannot feel
but the air must rush back between palms
into vacuums of praise.

People are clapping, sine-waves of clapping
that echo and drift in dry roars —
wind beating paper and sticks
in a tall, concrete cave.

Clapping to praise —
though the tenor's great fame,
and the cost, and the hands of their friends,
are what puppet them most.

Smiling, the tenor comes back
to accept and accept.

Outside or backstage
the clapping is mindless and frightening
like movements of peoples.
Mindless, and void: symbol,
like chevrons or lipstick;
verb from the mad, clumsy tongues
of perceptions of power.

Where did the heart — its delight — disappear?
This is not praise, it's exchange:
outside the women wait coyly with legs;
men plot to crawl, or exploit.

How can we share our response —
to delight,
(to despair?)

All verbs bear contracts and guns:
all else is adverb;
all adverb, lace.

# TOUCH

You cannot just walk up to someone and touch:
touch isn't free;
touch is exchange, it expects.
First, you must pay for some.
Then, you must maintain set roles —
or your access might stop.

Once you have got rights,
then most people feel, that's enough,
just to have some nearby —
taken for granted,
or hot and unconscious:
brutal, and clumsy,
or casual, like winding the clock.

Where is its art-form?

Why do we do it so badly?
So ungracious, sly?

Not walking, children,
through bright, starlit caves,
but butting each other with needs
on the floor of some kraal?

## ANDREW LANSDOWN

# A GOOD NIGHT

The mulies are in the harbour,
shoals of them, teeming unseen
in the opaque sea.  On the wharf,
in rubber boots and yellow raincoats,
a team of professional fishermen
lure the fish with food and light.
They have hung a lantern, hissing
incessant warning, just above
the quilted surface of the quiet water;
and they have strewn pollard —
the pollen grains, the yeasty smell —
on the water, below the lamp,
above the submerged net — an iron hoop
looped with mesh, long and tapering
like a wind-sock.  Near the net,
a ship shifts uneasily.  Its rope,
a catenary from prow to bollard,
strains and straightens.  Bilge-water
spouts from the hull.  On the wharf,
an enormous, enclosed conveyor-belt
rolls on its gantry.  Grain
cascades into the hold.  Behind
the ship, winnowed by the wind
and stretching as far as the shining
of the harbour lights, barley husks
form a yellow slick on the black
water.  Between the lamp and the net
the mulies, the bait-fish, swirl
like long-bodied moths.  At a command,
the men hoist the net.  It is a crucible
bubbling with molten silver.
Poured out, the fish separate
into small, oblong ingots.  A young man

smooths them into shallow crates,
ready for freezing.  But the fish
are not ready.  Frenzied,
they flick and twist, scales flying off
like sequins from a silver purse.
Their gills gape, the red frills
clogged by air.  Their mouths gasp,
transparent lips extended
like trumpets, blaring, "O!  O!"
The conveyor-belt and the bilge-pump
drone a duet to drown Death's reveille.
Wake up!  O!  O!  Our mortality!
The ship's rope heaves and relaxes.
In a child's hand, a line twitches
like a caught nerve.  In the crates,
the fish have gone off the boil
and lie eternally still.  The men
lower the net again.  "Gonna be a good
night," smiles one man, his hair
spangled with scales, like confetti.

MARK MILLER

# SOMEWHERE IN CENTRAL AUSTRALIA

Rattling,
shaking through dust
in the old truck —

in the back
with empty petrol barrels
two aborigines:

a young mother
and her daughter
crying

scratching the red
welts of her skin.

The truck shakes on,
the earth rumbles.

In the rear-vision mirror
the sky has strangely
clouded over —

The daughter wails.
I push down harder
on the pedal —

I am my father.

It is 1953.

## SUDESH MISHRA

# DETAINEE

*for Krishna Datt*

Images intensify in prison;
Time is a grid through which a turf of sky
Blazes at me. Every fifth hour I rest
An arm across these four rods. Three days
And I have learnt what sages understand
With age: be it bars or beads telling
Is wisdom. "Sir," the guard calls out softly,
Pushing through steel-ribs a bowl of dhal.
Why the aberration, I snidely ask,
Pointing to his aqua-watch — the closed cell
And open sea both trap a nerveless moment;
Outside bars and inside reefs a witless
Barracuda grinds its teeth. All around
Toady fish applaud. From the sixth row seeps
The dregs of a song: *I did it my way.*
The guard speaks: "Was a pupil of yours, Mr Datt,
Grammar '74." Hobnailed boots retreat.
Who'd have foretold that I could teach so much,
I, who am now instructed to drink from
An iron crucible, rinse the heart's sour gall?
Teachers trade in knowledge, only pupils
Get wise — but who the teacher, who the taught?
Each graffito, each oath, conveys a truth
Most dailies refute.
                          So here I am again,
Balding mouthpiece for B-section inmates,
Keeping tradition by penning on the wall,
Between "Fear was Here" and "Brown St., Brotherhood,"
A tribute to those unknown instructors:
*There's no prison, save in the demagogic heart.*

# A GOD FOR MAN

Goodmorning God.
Preacherman say you allabout allatime
so this make me think bout you
this onegod.    One.
Preacher say you make man your image
like you is made.
(He not tellame who made you).
This mighty thing he say but
make no sense for me.

I see man drunk outside this pub
his legs like legs on animal
born new.    This way.    That way.
His face has lines like rainwashed rocks,
his eyes they dead it seems.
No life inem no more.
Forever forgotten all they ever seen.
Is he like you?

When lubra lies by riverbank,
flies crawling bout her mouth
with empty bottle in her hand
I cry inside.
Is she like you onegod
this black who looks for dreams
in poison drink?

You in everyone preacher say.
In him.  In me.
In all living thing.
You every place.
You onegod who knows all things to know
but I not understand

how you feel bout wars onegod
when men kill women
their babies by their side.
You hear their screams,
their crying.
You see-em live.  You see-em dying.

This makes no sense for me.
I think you not make man like this.
Maybe man made you?
Man made you in his image
to make his self feel good!

Standing high on mountain
I feel you near,
allabout like preacher say.
Allabout.
But not like man.
I taste you in my mouth
sweet as wild honey
found in tree.

Looking down in valley
I small like ant
but you are there.
I feel you onegod inside me.
Not like me.
Not like me at all.
This makes you
God.

I stand by midden
on seashore.
Shells of ancestor feastings
lie from yesterdays tucker.
White egret sways her bill
in shallow water.
Here also I feel you near.
Not this God man made for men

but you as you be
before all men
before this world began
before Rainbow Serpent
                    came
                          from
                                  sky.

This magic is all aroundme
not blackman magic
or whiteman words
but humming music
in my heart
in singing trees
in currawong calling.
Even ants stand still
between these beats of time.

I hold my breath
to listen in magic silence
while heart lies still.
Something is here.
Something preacher not know.

God?          God?
Like drinking water
I drink in air.
It brings me back to life.

Every thing comes alive again
allatime running flying leaping calling.
Leaves dance in summer sun
while cockatoos scream
from fading sky.
Cicadas screech in tall trees.
Wallabies eat dry grass.

This air is everywhere
allabout us.
Inside.        Outside.
Giving life to all living thing.
This air makes life inside us.
It gives us life
and takes us away.
Man is in Gods image allright
but not like preacher sees it.
Man is in God.  God is in man.
I take big breath so air rushes in.

Kookaburra begins to laugh.
Laughing.           Laughing.
I laugh withim.
Soon we all laughing
whole world laughing at big big joke.
Then I dance on hilltop
pounding feet on naked earth,
breathing dust between my toes,
crying to Mirramurra . . .
Comendance.      Comendance.
This way we dance with onegod.
The world.  Mirramurra.  And me.

PENELOPE NELSON

# ADVENTURES IN NEW FRENCH FEMINISM

for Margaret Coombs

"The hysteric suffers from reminiscence." — Freud.


Once a month through the seventies
my copies of Vogue and Women's Liberation Journal
arrived in the same mail.
Now we dutifully come to this conference
Feminine/Masculine/Representation
or have I transposed the sexes?
No one says the words without stumbling.

Don't go to a psychoanalyst to try to understand yourself
it's expensive and time consuming,
get a fortune-teller to tell you more expertly
or a conversation with a friend is better still.

Language is not patriarchal, but
the language of the dominant discourse is.
Where do we go from here, mes amies?
The couple from Paris
the comedy team
he proposes, she opposes
he lectures, she interrupts
he is balding, bespectacled, lucid, a figure of authority
she has a fiercely intelligent face, long nose, grey eyes,
floaty chiffon scarves, dramatic earrings
and, of course, French cosmetics.
The glamour could be his or hers or unisex,
or a component of their double act,
personifying the conference title.
No one here would be so naive

as to use a word like natural.
What does woman want?
He says, she doesn't know herself.
She says, Everything.
The caption of the cartoon has Freud asking the question
his patient lying on a couch
blindfolded and gagged.
A scream which cannot be heard
is nevertheless still a scream.
Que veut la femme?
Is it a market research question —
is the answer Valium? Arpège? Diamonds?
Promise her anything
Sing 'em muck.
Love is . . .
giving what you haven't got
to someone who doesn't want it anyway.

She says Nothing my lord
He says Nothing shall come of nothing
her hesitations put into question
coherent notions of truth.
Freud could not conquer his mother
so he invented psychoanalysis.
Masturbation is forbidden by the one who inititated it.

The archaic dimension of language is the maternal.
When I wrote that story about my mother tongue
a clever man denied it was écriture féminine.
Writing in mother's milk
as recommended by Helene Cixous
would put authenticity beyond doubt
but as that sugary smell turned sour
and words faded like invisible ink
would we really be further ahead?

Jacqueline has just given a lecture
about a romantic novella
sent as a homoerotic love token

between Freud and Jung
who rave about Gradiva, the heroine.
Mentioning Lou Salome
she reminds us of the latent homosexual bond
between two men who love one woman.
When she gives a copy of her own book to me
what am I to say?
Feminism and etiquette collide.
"Je suis boulversée" is excessive,
not to say flirtatious,
while "Thank you so much" is too British.
Is it OK to tell her I'm grateful?

In the psychoanalyst's novel,
the heroine, a psychoanalyst,
goes on holiday to Italy
with half a dozen other psychoanalysts
one of whom, the hostess,
confides in the heroine about a wild affair.
A young man named Franz
son of an Austrian pianist
on the verge of a breakdown
is rescued during a downpour
either out of professional concern
or self-deluding seduction.
This is all told in French,
the subtext, a German novella,
provides it with points of departure.

The daughter-mother bond of the pre-Oedipal phase
of attachment to the mother
is inexorably repressed
destined, he says, to resist words;
destined, she says, to resist psychoanalysis.

Remembering in dreams the mind before words,
a web, a loom, a pattern puzzle
dangling bedraggled before me.
Just before waking I draw connecting lines,

weave threads, mend gaps, find shapes.
At death, does the pattern hold,
or like the kaleidoscope does it shift and reshift
forever dazzles of symmetry
or are cosmic computers somehow generating
subconscious Mandelbrot sets?

Leaving the chairman's office I note down
the paintings on his walls
a sunrise over the sea
a surveyor hammering something on a tree near a lake
a bushfire
a waterfall
a snarling tiger.
They won't promote me around here.

If the body is a writing surface
and pain the great mnemonic,
if consciousness is the effect not the cause
of the inscription of flesh
what would the experts from Paris say about
the father of my childhood friend
who used to send her out to cut the plumsticks
for him to beat her with?
He used a red plastic ruler on me, going easy,
I wasn't his flesh and blood,
but that word **plumstick** scars my mind with fear
the way it scarred her flesh.

It's her birthday today.
I ask her mother how she is (she lives abroad)
She gives a short dry laugh
— Not happy, but what's new?

JOHN NEWTON

# NARRATIVE

I wanted you both at once, I thought: I wanted
you, I wanted this, I imagined that
somehow as the valley shut behind us you & I would be
close as for the first time, foxgloves
showing us the pink of their pouches, deltas of ducks' wings,
openings, November in the blood.

Out past the end of the paper road you nursed
the vehicle solicitously.  The cocky
sat perched on his sawbench & flashed you
a smile with his blue eye
tooth when he spoke to you, following
the movement of your lips as he listened to you, throat

bobbing, reddening, turkey-necked with lust.
In the sawdust two cockerels were trying to
tread one another.  Sing out, he told us, if there's anything
you need, & the invitation troubled me
subtly, & fell in with me as we slogged our way inland.
Ahead of us too there were thunderheads now

thrusting up their mushrooming columns of ice, & the dirty
dishwater colour of snowmelt in the river.
From nowhere a deer appeared, its headless body
tumbling end over end in the current
while a figure on the far bank ran downstream beside it
& a pretty little eye dog, boulder-hopping

gamely.  Your heart was not in it, I could
tell by the way you kept putting the miles so determinedly
behind you.  Making camp under a lump of morraine
we couldn't find anything to say to one another.

Night fell & still I could not get near you.
I lay awake, shivering, talking in my mind to you,

listening to your downy blue sleeping bag
shifting, whispering, purring, breathed into
by your body.  A mouse drowned, thrashing in a dirty billy,
wanting something, dumbly, that it couldn't have.
I woke to find its burred pelt floating in the scum.
Your sleeping bag was cold.  You were gone.

Crawling out after you, I called & called
but there was no sign of you, just this vista you were
missing from: flashing from an outcrop
of rock, a parrot's wing; mangy blond tussock
whispering; spaniards rubbing their spines together;
tutu, its poison-asparagus suckers cocked.

# BARK CANOE

for Sandy Atkinson

The cut takes a known shape,
long oval of repetitive metal-blows on bark,
till you see what will fall from the tree
as a living prow.
The tomahawk works on round the edge
chopping back to hardwood.
This long corky coat, much heavier
than you dreamed bark could be,
floats on a film of slippery sap-flow,
worn loosely for this one month in Spring.
(A week late, and the bark has shrunk, clings
tight as corpse-skin to its tree).
Now we push and pry coaxing
our tree to grant wishes;
a shaped branch like a Dutch hoe
pushes under the sheet, plowing upwards; each thrust
pumps up the bark, just short of splitting

— then woos it loose, with sounds of soft tearing.
All morning our wedges work, straining
to free this boat marooned on a tree,
levering, hammering, willing it
all not to rip or part,
propping, peeling and forcing
the moist shapeable rind
that will ever afterwards hang together.

Then so slowly
while ignorant ants go crazy
round sap-oozing edges,
the long side of a sheet ridges outward for good
— all this violence rests on such gentleness —
and the bark canoe lowers slowly
onto a dozen willing hands.

JAN OWEN

from CROSSING THE PIAZZETTA

# THE CAMPANILE

"You seem a little sad, Madame?"
Should I have turned away?
I liked the cut of his coat
the quirk of his head
and his moustached smile
the missing tooth on one side
gave him a gently piratical look.
And yes, I was sad
a surfeit of cold pale glass
and glittering masks
and . . . the mist perhaps.
"Just a short walk"
his arm already in mine
his steps paced right.
Ah, that seductive style, that plausible charm
a Venetian art.
Timing's the trick
deftness, patience, then
one quick move
the glassworker's technique.
You can watch them on Murano
twirling a glowing molten mass
drawing a liquid filament out
blowing a bubble sudden as
that
with the red-gold furnace roaring behind.

So we crossed the Piazzetta
and followed the waterfront
past the fringe cafés
and their clutter of empty chairs

faded confetti from Carnivale
stuck in the cobbles still
the carousel men and the peanut stands
doing poor trade
and the slop of animals at a trough
was only waves at the wall
and the out-of-season complaints
just seagulls slanting in
tugs and gondolas riding it out.

Giuglio had been retrenched
from the Finance Ministry
which was "corrupt."
"Italian politics?" a shrug to the gods.
He would go to Germany, to friends
paint landscapes, make ships in bottles,
open a shop maybe
his hands already up and away.
Going back
we talked of tides and floods
took coffee at Mario's
strong as a shot in the arm.
Mario watched from behind
his white china stack.
Featureless, polished as butlers
the porphyry lions outside
looked straight ahead.
Deeper now, the pools in the Square
the sea welling up through the grates
with little guttural cries.
No wave over the wall
in Venice the flood comes up from below
catches you unawares.

And Giuglio showed me the High-water Mark
on the Campanile.
Past our waists.
"Arrivederci, then."
He flung his arms wide

then drew me in
and kissed me again and again
with the Campanile at his back
(absurdly apt I thought even then)
and again, warm and hard
and I might have stayed
that questioning look, that smile
and the water rising steadily, fast
but I caught my breath
and pushed apart.      Done.
The last brittle snap of cooling glass
that cuts off dolphin, fish
or some more airy problematical form.
I looked back once and waved.

# THE CANDLE

And then went in to a pine room full of sun.
This was the year of *szabadság, demokrácia,*
        and it was late afternoon,
The fir tree lifting, lifting and scraping
        bear's claws at the pane
As the Russian units went to it behind the hill
        dull thuds, a failure sound
        two a minute, to use up their shells.
And this was early in 89
        after a winter of little rain
        the units beginning to pull out.
It was the month before they knocked down the wall,
        the Hungarians that is,
With the East Germans, Czechs, and Rumanians grinding their
teeth.
And we sat in the room by a shelf of poetry
        most of it Pound,
        the floor swept clean,
Warm bread, Mozart, and five point Tokay wine.
And Carl, he was a teacher at the school,
        had rice and basil chicken hot, just done;
His thesis would be
        "'Contrapuntal technique in the Cantos' —
        the whole ragbag
      *shining and silvery as fresh sardines.*"
His fingers called oboe, cello, first violin,
       *"then light air, under saplings,*
*the blue banded lake under aether,"*
Coaxing the grace-notes back to thought.
And Pound's cane chair in Venice was curved and deep
        with a wide weave like a poem or a cage;
We'd heap the clean clothes up high
        a fresh linen smell escaped all round.
*"Love, gone as lightning,*
    *enduring 5000 years."*

Through Almádi now, the almond trees
would be dim perfume,
A light wind skimming the pewter tang of the lake
and sheering the silver away.
*"Shall the comet cease moving*
*or the great stars be tied in one place!"*
It was already night.
Carl shut the book,
lit the fat yellow candle
and put Scarlatti on.
We buttered more rolls and finished the wine.
The soft gold of the flame
was an adequate light.

# HERENDI PORCELAIN

Bródy Sándor U. 17, second courtyard, no. 1:
I took the room.
Anna worked from home
         (dark shadows under her eyes
            and a cough)
on a racketty black tank turret
        that typed
            machine gun rounds
               and stopped

only for cigarettes
        Maci, the cat
          and coffee
            coffee.
She'd bring mine in a deep scalloped cup and saucer
         patterned with clover leaves
           round the rim
             an elegant thing.
"Herendi porcelain,"
         the last of a set of eight.
The rest?

        A hand wave
          new lights, food, the rent.

Pawned and gone.
I drained it carefully
        breathed it safe down.
"Listen."

        A tap of the spoon and it sang
          the voice of a lady
            swirling her green crinoline.
"This one I keep!"

        Her sisters, seven little pawns
         swept off the board
           not much is ever redeemed.

Anna
> I see you still
>> with the cat
> that infernal machine
>> the apricot brandy
>>> too many cigarettes
and the Herendi cup held high
>> your finger cocked like a lady
>>> at Them *("a szarházi népség!")*
bearing it up and on
> the survivor
>> towards the back line
>>> a Queen.

Not the cup Anna!

# METRO

Buskers, somewhere at Châtelet —
their plainsong sounding the corridors for sky
raised transept, nave, and vault,
flooding them with unearthly light,
a silvery puzzlement the soul must feel
roaming artery, neurone, bowel.
At Tuileries a small drunk man lurched on,
slumped down and breathed in my hair.  The train's
precipitate birth hurled us along
a darkness beyond the reach of song.
"Un homme seul, tu comprends."  I looked away
hoping he wouldn't vomit or cry.
"Tu comprends pas la solitude?"
He kept it up well past Concorde:
"English?  I understand English.  Look,"
he searched his coat for a paper-back —
it was Gulliver clawing out at us
from the grip of a leering giantess.
He followed a black girl at L'Etoile
but missed the exit.  I went up in the spill
of feet to a rush of wintry air
and the Champs Élysées plane trees sifting stars.
You could take wrong turns and trains for hours
down there — the labyrinth breeds on emptiness,
claims any outcast.  Sometimes the choice is just
two different ways of being lost,
soul and seul are both importunate.
But I wish I'd smiled; these words come too late.

# THIRD CLASS HOTEL

Leicester Court was misrun
by five nationalities;
the shower was cold, the lift stalled,
and the key wouldn't turn.
On the second day I complained
and they sent the handyman up.
It was him again,
dark eyes and a soft moustache
too melancholy for anyone but a Pole.
The problem was not the key,
the lock was worn;
it worked three quarters in,
he showed me how.
"Please. You try"
(his hand over mine):
the right fit, slight opposition,
an easing home,
and it opened sweet as a thought.
He nodded and smiled in that wry way
ideal and actual don't quite meet.
*And that's how you'd be. Yes.*
*Warm, sad-funny, precise,*
*with a sort of elusive grace*
*so even afterwards*
*telling when you were small*
*and the geese chased you up the cherry tree*
*on your uncle's farm,*
*you wouldn't be close,*
*the bed would be seven valleys wide,*
*distance would flute you away.*
It's a skill they learn in the Eastern bloc,
patching and fixing, making do;
also the indirect route, the absence game.
I can't revert to third person singular now;
thank you dear second person singular Pole
for the knack; it worked like a charm.

## GEOFF PAGE

# from *IMPROVISATIONS*

A gifted child
forgotten in a room
with sunlight and piano

the sound suspended glass
struck gently there
with satin mallets,

the right hand outlines
blues and fugues,
the left suggests

transparent chords.
It is a kind of
game with space,

the unheard equal
to the heard,
the composition

recomposed
each time more simple
than the last,

a texture of the
mind alone
where any moment now we know

applause will break the glass.

DOROTHY PORTER

from *AKHENATEN*

# MY FATHER'S BLACK HANDS

When the embalmers
    have finished with him
under the bandages
    my father's hands are black

he touched this chair
his thick finger traced
its enammelled gold,
he touched this alabaster bottle
absent-mindedly he played
with the smooth jaws
of its hippopotamus stopper
he liked it near him
when he was tired,
lots of toys
he had lots of toys
and he touched them all

years ago
he liked me near him
he touched my bare skull
I remember his soft tired hand

now
my father's hands are black.

# CEREMONY OF THE OPENING OF THE MOUTH

This last intimacy
with my father

this cracking open
his old mouth

has he many teeth left
for me
to break?

No breath on my hand.

The white sun.
My wet armpits.

Under all the lotions
under all the perfumes
I stink
worse
than my dead father.

He's a husk
they've gutted
and dried out
with salt

I should blow him away

then, in glory,
every dawn
I'll whisper him alive
I'll be his God
his thousand-fingered
paramour
touching him everywhere
with light

his mouth
I've broken his mouth

Daddy
    oh forgive me
    this indecency!

# SHE LEAVES HER THINGS

What sort of face
   is she wearing
   at the Northern Palace?

She's left behind
   all her cosmetics.
Even her tweezers.
Will my love be sprouting
   thick eyebrows?

Grow hideous, Nefertiti,
tumble in public
your hairy grief
like a performing dwarf.

Even Hapu.  The monkey pot.
Left him behind too.
I see the mark
   of your finger nail
in his kohl.

I stole him
   from my mother's chest,
we were still kids
   but your new breasts
      nudged me to it.

I'd like one like that,
   you said
so I pinched him.

Hapu
    we called him
after the smart little monkey
      who built temples
        for my father.

I'm not touching your things.

Not looking at myself
    in your mirror.

The sluts in my harem
    can have the lot.

# KRISTOPHER SAKNUSSEMM

# APPEARANCE VS. REALITY

I first saw those words
scratched in white chalk
on the murky green blackboard,
alongside phrases like
MAN'S INHUMANITY TO MAN.

While we wondered what colour
underwear she was wearing,
Miss DeJulio laboured
to teach us themes and
hidden meanings, never knowing
what we were really thinking.

Too skinny to be pretty, single,
and knee-deep in other people's children,
she scraped the short thick sticks
of hard white dust across the slate
each day, scarring PLEASE SAVE
in a hissing shriek of friction —
circling it for the janitor to read.

I don't know what became of her,
whether she found happiness
or grew fat — or whether she just faded
like the terms and definitions
she seemed intent upon carving
into the blackboard and our brains.

But I remember writing her a poem once,
which ended with the lines —
"Sometimes everything is exactly
as it seems.  Just as there are no

more wolves in England, except
in zoos or dreams."

I stood expectantly beside her desk,
studying her face as she read my words
and circled the part about the wolves
with a yellow Ticonderoga Number 2 pencil
gripped tight in her fine-boned hand.

It was the first time all year
I'd ever seen her even
on the brink of a smile.
But when she touched her face,
she left a trace of damp grey chalkdust
on her cheek.

# PHILIP SALOM

# DRIVING

We have put aside the airport and
the highways that sigh like jets
high up and falling upwards in the brain.
Now the air is milky: village light
stropped this morning from the cow and goat,
let calm into sequestering streets.
Driving through villages with
no pavements, where the gap between
the slab walls of shops and houses
is the light, is the road, like a peasant logic.
The air *is* milky.  The centuries
have fed upon it, and feed on it.
And we, passing through it,
so joyed up by it, by nothing less
than putting away, like breath,
the left side.  The air like milk
in village after village
siestered and absent, or there
an old woman scratching her hand
between houses which hold this air
like a member of the family.
We drive the right side, seeing
with this brain each village
like a film of muted colours,
the fields under smoke.

# FLORENCE SWUNG DOWN

Florence is religion.  My head goes white
thinking of Australia, our blue air
bleeding up like levitation.  Here the past
is kept weighed down by stone cathedrals
and the heavy sites of history.
A child, I marked my voices off
upon the stones, the rivers, the trees.
These were my imaginings, my alibis.

Florence is architecture full of alibis.
In pointing up weighed down
the medieval quilt of Europe.
And maybe, possibly, the guilt.
Guilt?  At a gallery it stops,
becomes the easiest of depths
so slow and gentle to the structures.
Wandering here I sink
like a sieve through water.

Here is genius, skill, the crucial
unexpectedness in things we know.
But slowly I can feel the cost
behind the model of heroics, the statue,
the canvas.  Dutch or Italian, the Duke
lifts inspiring fingers
as if under the hem of chosen whores.
And now, this arrogance lifts up
into the ozone, hurting even statues
to the skin.  Florence is soon
replacing them with copies.

I am taken by the metaphor
of thinners on the sooty walls
peeling back chiaroscuro
where it has grimed and aged, brown
onto the marble, brown onto the saints,

brown in the silent shadows of each canvas.
It washed the slovenly streets
like sewage, stank of the dying mouths
and stomachs of the poor, it stained
corruptly in the eyes of Borgias, it bled
among the violent soldiery of Florence.

When it is grime softening to bruises
on Da Vinci's tender, mind-lit
skins: it shows the throat of his friend
strangled on Cesare's, his patron's, orders.
Genius is made a flunky.

## SWUNG

I talk to a Byzantine Madonna,
ask her how she tolerates her clones
in their blessed hundreds, their halos
saying it straight off: oh Gaudy Gaudy!
The only Christ I've never seen
is fat. Thank God there are some black.

I turn my back on tourists
(like a panel closing . . . )
as if by doing this
I taste the air as halfly as Lucretia
ate the apple she had poisoned
to one side only of the knife.
I wish to fly, I fold my wings.

What has been dug up is caged off,
excavation as a lair for unseen
beasts: inside this hole, the Roman air
that was boiling, air full
of stink and steam, of cuts and anthrax
bubbling in the skin. This was
the dying air, the tanner's pit. Air

cramped as tetanus by the cold.
(Terror opens its mouth against a wall
somewhere, always.)  Here I feel voice
sinking like a sieve through me,
saying don't count this off.
It shakes the panels near my hand.

All the statues line up in the square
outside, horse and human hearts,
convulsing in the white.
Here I begin to hear the voices,
see the lights, one among the many
of artist, partisan, audience,
I play along, ahead on years,
suspect or witness at this identification.
I rub my chin and point,
say yes, this one, this one,
to every one of them.  Keep the air.

MICHAEL SHARKEY

from *PICTURES AT AN EXHIBITION*

# *The Breakaway*, Tom Roberts, 1891

Art Gallery of South Australia

This is a snap of me on Phar Lap.
The untidy grey things are the sheep.
If you look closely, two F-One-Elevens
have just had the quince on the ridge.
Funny how Ektachrome always makes
Hyde Park look dull.
And I fell off the horse.

# The Railway Station,
# Arthur Streeton, 1893

Art Gallery of New South Wales

Vickery's bookshop was shut
by the time I arrived,
and we missed the last tram
to the Royal Easter Show.
All of the kooris said Honky Go Home
at the pub, and the cops moved us on.
Sydney on Sunday's no fun.
In the Park, a professor of German
came up and read poems and offered
our Lucy some help with her orals.
The train home was late.
Life is always getting off at Redfern.

# *Sausage Valley*,
# Frank Crozier, France 1916

Australian War Memorial, Canberra

This is the triumph of Modernist thought:
antinomians all, we lie here in the mud
and no semblance of home,
and the moral elite has gone mad.
Our Captain, as young as he was,
was the best of us all:
as the wounded withdrew
he bore three rifles, said "Not a word
to the brass." Hard men wept
when he staggered and fell.
What is left to rely on?
The Press? And our wives?
Oz brought a letter from home,
from the brother at school,
and I wrote "If you love me,
don't come," and next thing the young fool
is among reinforcements: he grins.
And good night. And they want me to write.
No use explaining to those who wave flags
or extol what they think it all means.
Not a word from the ones who go back:
they keep mum or they crack.
Here in this snap you see cordite and gas:
something real. Shrapnel plays into the mud.
People once lived on the flat.
We've gone modern, and scraped off all that.

# *Circe,*
# Bertram Mackennal, 1892

National Gallery of Victoria

Need I remind you
no effort was needed
by me to turn men into swine.
Do-it-yourself is the name of the game
they're performing down there on the base.
Look at them go at it,
like some dull epic of blonde Californians,
impossibly long on the job.
And their eyes: nothing home;
and their women: this lift does not go
all the way to the top.

Once this was all you required
to turn every man to art critic: observe,
they would cry, how he captures
the fullness, the form, the exquisite etceteras.

Whatever the coil at the feet might suggest,
and the pose and the snakes
(Mister Freud, Mister Jung, are you home?)
and the winged chappy dozing off
having had his fling at *Hollywood Babylon* sports
with that mob at my feet,
I was paid to stand still.

Thanks to a century gravid with perving men
reading the dirty bits you can observe
my hair done by the Hairdressing Salon's
gay President while I just wait
for my nails to dry out and get dressed.

Stuck in a room full of guards and alarms
and dull landscapes I've time to reflect
that all art history's bunk,
all mythology's junk,
and the rest's gynaecology, yes.

# *Lacquer Room,*
# Grace Cossington Smith, 1936

### Art Gallery of New South Wales

In the cafe, I listened today:

"His wife's coming back to him,
what should I do?  A friend
in the army has volunteered
to Luger her.  I admit it cheered
me quite a bit to consider that end
to the problem.  I mean it; it isn't a whim."

I drank my wine, ate pasta mista
(excellent sauces), became attention:

"Jealousy's the devil's invention,"
I told her straight, "I wouldn't fester
about the dilemma behind locked doors,
but bearing in mind . . . " — "What would you have done?"
"Give her the business end of the gun."

# The Foundation of Perth, G. Pitt Morison

### Art Gallery, Perth

Here's another gubba picture:
someone's got a message stick
they call a telescope.
You look through that
and everything you see
is Torrens Title.  Magic, eh?
The missus is holding an axe
for protection against the bloke
who will ringbark the dreaming.
A convict gub's cleaning
the tucker-bag up while her back's turned.
Two fellows are saying
the setting's just right for a pub.
All the ghosts with guns wear red,
and the clouds are moving out
towards the sea.  The headman's got
a cheque in his hands that'll bounce
and no one's singing.

# *Schoolgirl Standing in Street*, Charles Blackman, 1953

Warrnambool Art Gallery

I'll go mad when I grow up.
My aunties did, and Mummy's in
Germaine Greer's latest novel.

Nobody's looking at me in this picture,
a change from what happens
each time I get in at this hour.

You could wait all night for a bus
and then it'd go the wrong way.
But nobody believes it.

I'm glad I can't see what's behind me.
The things people do.  Roses grow
below the ground as well: did you know that?
The world's carnivorous.

# The Works, Yallourn, Ethel Spowers, 1933

Latrobe Valley Arts Centre

Something I like about this:
I was dreaming of waterfowls,
when I looked up, and there was
the railway-line, coal-heaps
and powerlines stretching away to the sky.
Well of course I'd read Ginsberg
and Corso and Zen and all that,
and I knew that I'd paint it.

Over the hill the conveyor belt sat
like a Russian Constructivist dream
someone knew I would love.

I sing the factory electric,
power, speed.  I put the horse in the shade
when my teacher remarked "You want scale,"
for a joke.  You can't get away
from the human shape, animals,
anywhere: who'd want to try?
Flock of homesick ibis
flying night and day to their nests . . .
I forget the rest.

CRAIG SHERBORNE

# THE LOPPER

A Ferris-wheel chair spinning its backwards many years
To stop down from the sky and pick boys with handfuls up.

Divided from the ground and equal to trees,
Breaking stressed windtips, the cherry-picker skids
Its outset away from the pinnacle of watchers' upturned
Hands sun-shielding, visoring leaves from their faces
Shrinking to an audience.

Slowly as weakness moves, unsteady as strength
The stretched neck's windpipe of hydraulic cord
Clears its breath, the tub rocks twice and tries
To rest itself along branch-sprouting branches
The lopper unforms with quick calculations
And drops safely askew down his height's
Deep well to the ground.

My eyes browed with my hands, my scalp itchy
From damp dust I await my time below where fresh logs
Thud. Hearing the choked chain blade-off clean.
Watching through less leaves the sun burn down westward
One stove-length at a time.
An hour or more before the man grows tired. He eases
The gears and rides the soft hissing fall.

He passes me ropes, the harness and his saw,
My hands full of serious weight, I take my turn.

ANDREW TAYLOR

# IN THE LANDSCAPE OF THE BROS. GRIMM

I've come home to a landscape
not my own.  Towers of grass
crane over me and the air
is always twilight, a misty avenue
of birdsong that will never sleep
before I do.
                    This may be Eden
the picturebook childhood that now
adult, I venture into unguided
by innocence.  Yet though I see
aphis blacken the new shoots
of cherrytrees and slugs patrol
the tall stinging gangways of nettles, this
is untainted by the timid
evaporating hopes of my own
childhood.
                    There, grasping a nettle
the Children's Encyclopaedia way
left a red sizzling weal across my hand,
and since the sun rose back to front
I never could find my bearings
from lichen in a wood.  There were
no woods, where I grew up, and precious little
bush either, just an expanse for sheep
and indecipherable scrawl
of sea where it drew the line
at our venturing out yet refused to abide
its own side of the border, foraying in
as bitter salt wind.

But if I lie here
by the appletree, when the helicopters
each 8 pm have faded away
to the army base, I can re-enter
stories my sister would read to me,
the light low, the door closed, as
hand in hand, with hesitant voice and low
we wandered toward the gingerbread house
of Europe, in its magic wood.

# IN THE RHINE VALLEY

for Gisela and Ingo

With the landscape unfolding like pages
of an illustrated history, I'm struck
by how new it all is.  Castles
cloisters, jousting meadows, Charlemagne's
favourite domain — they're scratched
onto something far older, more subtle
and less impatient to be noticed.
                              Hills
plunge to a river plain.  Among vines
and fringes of poplar the river divides
between tree-lined islands.  It flows
from the icy Alps towards a sunless sea
far north.  Small bands of people with flints
and embers followed it, floating at times
on hollowed logs.  Many drowned.
When the river flooded, as it often does,
they and their reedy huts were washed away.
Later came Legions, then an array
of Alemani, Franks, and the beginning
of dynasties.  Ours too.  Whatever they found
they left it changed.  A ring of stones
a cache of plaited gold, the cultivation
of grapes, the etherial echoing
of plainsong in an icy basilica,
the railway, later the autobahn, cruise boats
and the Frankfurt flightpath.  The Rhine
takes them all in.  It's a great
sluice of history, of human time
where the pulse of Europe is still felt
as riverboats circle at dusk against the flow
and moor for the night, facing the source, upstream.

Riverboats know that history's
not simply people. It's made by rivers
and they're not to be trusted. Moved
only by rain and snow, and fallen from folds
of the cooling earth, they carve steep hills
to occasional plains of silt. And vines
drilled to attention over it cannot conceal
— despite the clutch of their roots
in the shaley slopes, and the lemony wink
of this Romer of riesling — the glacial
drift of this valley, the casual hunch
of the Taunus behind, untouched by our fear,
and the knowledge that when we go, whoever and where,
the river will flow as ever, and couldn't care.

CAMPBELL THOMSON

# from *NORTH HITCH*

for Goobalathaldin

"Chance meetings along the road, these too have their secret
meaning" — Aeskylos

## Canto 3

A girl to cast a long blond smiling line
For a fish eyed hauler to strike his brakes
And then you walk out of the bush is fine
Fraud when it works, but mostly it just makes
For a lung full of diesel.  This guy must
Just have paid off his rig and felt his luck
Had changed for at the turning circle dust
Swirled round and I was sucked into his truck.
He had few words for several hours and then
He only spoke to keep awake.  This is his tale.


At 3 am the Hume Highway lights
Up the sky . . . the Bennies sometimes fail:
You drift across the lane, your bumper bites
A dozy car in half . . . You can float along
On automatic pilot, cook your books
And what's the point? A few more bucks.  That song —
You know it? "Prisoner of the white lines . . ." Looks
Like there's a prang somewhere. Faarkk . . . You know, a real
Shambles, road turns into a Christmas tree
Of cat's eyes and rubies . . . sometimes you feel
Part of a snake stretched Melbourne to Sydney . . .
Old girl gets up-tight when they flash the news,

Reckons it might be me . . . You married mate?
(Pause)
      No.
                My three kids sometimes refuse
To recognise me; hope I'm not too late
To-night to see them.  Early bloody start
To-morrow too — deposit on this house blew
All our stash so up at sparrow's fart
To load . . . Our land's out west, it's real grouse, too.

I look around the gizmos in his cab
And wonder what comes next — a video?
A spa?  A car phone so his wife can blab
To him on the way to the Leisure Show?
A microwave to defrost frozen pies
Or roast the cat?  A water bed, no doubt,
Or tennis court.  Consumer paradise:
A supermarket mall with no check out.

Where the road forks he drives right and I'm left
Cornered; but music on my Walkman kills
The kerb-side blues as J.S.  Bach's deft
Fingers trill, Giacomo Puccini fills
The verge with **Tosca's** frills; Van Morrison
Wails **On the Right Side of the Road**; Jarret's
Ad-libbing **Koln**, Dylan drones along on
**Highway 61, The Roller Girl** gets
Grooving into Dire Straits, Coloured Girls
**Only 40 Miles from Saturday Night**
Whirl to Planxty's plaintive fifing skirls
While Black Watch Pipes and Drum's **Black Bears** delight
In battle Verdi's **Requiem Mass** for Marvin Gaye
Who **Heard It on the Grape Vine** that Ella
Fitzgerald finds it **Too Darn Hot** today
To trot.  Leporello tots that fella
Don Giovanni's lays — **I Was Only**
**Nineteen**, had hardly tried out my refrain;
Wiling away flies, fazed, wasted, lonely
The sun's hot stanzas fry my scrambled brain.

# Canto 4

A Ford toots and my freeway concert ends,
A Marlborough Man with Texas bootlace tie,
Longhorn moustached, a hairy paw extends
And air conditioning puts out the sky.
Cigarette stubbed, jettisoned, he turned
And said:
                    I have a business call to make
Along the road.  A former client's burned
His place down.  I'm the receiver, might take
Me some time to sort it out, is that all
Right?
                    I nod and count the telegraph poles
Pan by without a word.  A Rugby football
Lies beneath my feet.  He smiles,
                                        Kicked some goals
With that last week . . . Follow the League?
                                        More keen
On Union.  Played a bit until the knee
Packed up.
                    I see him: a scragging has-been
Gouging in rucks the referee can't see
While I dream up the touchline, swerve right past
The fullback, trip a flailing flanker's hand
To spin in a heap and fail in the last
Move of the game to score a try . . . We land
With a jolt in a hole by the gate.
                                        Geez,
What stinks —
                    he holds a hankie to his nose:
Thousands of charred Red Roosters shoot the breeze
With stench, a holocaust of fowl —
                                        It goes
To show how crazy some blokes get when they
Go down the tube.  This little blaze will
Cost the Company heaps.  You'd think he'd play
The game.  It makes me sick.  I'd bloody kill

The bastard if he hadn't shot through.  Not
A cent to pay the bloody legal bill.

      (With rising gorge he has to stop.)
                               Know what?
Next week the new boss up in Tokyo
Is coming through and I've got all these tips
Stuck on the books not worth a yen.  And no
Soft timber here the Nips can trash for chips.

We skirt around the coops of cindered chooks,
Kentucky fried before their time.  He punts
An empty can at the charred shacks and looks
Up for the Bankrupts' Patron Saint and grunts.

He drops me at a nowhere roundabout
In dairy land with not a car in sight.
It is so still, so quiet I have to shout
To know it's real.  This puts the cows to flight.
My footsteps echo winding up the hill
From lush, green paddock lawns into the shade
Of flowering gums where treble Bell Birds fill
The nave with sounds no choir ever made.
Breathless, I shed my pack and sit and sip
Some water from a creek and munch some bread.
No wine but a fine lunch.  I slowly dip
My head into the pool.  The world is dead.

# Canto 7

Rusty white combi van slews in the dust
And stops.  I'm dragged from dreams, sprint up the track
He drawls behind a fag
                              Gold Coast or bust
O.K.?  Then chuck ya ruck sack in the back.
Ignore the dog, he likes a wog to chew
For lunch.  (Laughs, coughs.) Just outa school?

Nah.  Went south to escape the wet.  And you?

I'm from **Katoomba**, run the local pool.

The grinning dingo slavers in my ear,
Two grimy kids agog sit at my side,
Their hassled Mum throws me a wary sneer:
Her driving and I'd still be there, stir-fried.
We spurn the coast.  The inland road unzips
A frizzled, chapped flatness shimmered with wheat;
Too dull for I-spy and tricks for long trips
And too hot to sleep.  Only yarns might beat
The grizzles: Mulga Bill, Dot, Clancy,
Ginger Mick, tales of colonial boys
That they'd not heard before and do not fancy.
So, no strummed Banjo only blood and noise,
Raiders of lost rhymes, a video game
Of space invaders in our glass cocoon.
The screen goes black.  I steer their eyes and name
The Southern Cross.  Our fingers shoot the moon.
We park in **Goondiwindi** near a pub
Next to the Anzac Memorial Park.

Ah, Greta love, um, find the kids some grub
And fix the tent before it gets too dark.
We'll see you in a jiff.  Just a quick beer —
To clear the throat.

Get pissed and crawl back late,
I'll have you jokers.
                                    She'll be jakes, dear,
See you soon . . . Thank Christ for that.  Let's go mate,
Sink a schooner or two.  Can't take bein' cooped
Up with the meat and screamin' veg all day.
Besides this road'd try the Pope.  I'm pooped.

Few prop the bar.  Their eyes look up and say
Get lost and stay that way.  Four blacks play pool
On tattered felt in cowboy hats.  They pay
No stares to us with segregated cool.

My shout.  Whaddaya do then son?  You're not
A student?
                                    Nah.  Gave it the flick.  I fish
That dirty bath, the Gulf.  My boss has got
His boat outa dry dock; the prawns'll wish
The cyclone tipped us: when we're on the boil
Bananas flip so quick that down below
The freezers overflow . . . This wet could spoil
Our chance to make some serious dough though.

I get to fish out dive-bombed kids half-drowned
And test the piss for water.  It's a job.

The eighth or ninth beer elbowed, hoisted, downed,
We're friends for life when from nearby a sob
Lets rip a chuckle, laugh then whooping hoot —

**kooKooKOOKOOKOOKOOKAAKAAKaakaa**

THROW THE BLOODY KAFFIR OUT, THE BOONG
GALOOT!

My friend's demand assaults the bar.  The blacks,
Game over, doff their hats and saunter out.

He does that when he wins, the barman cracks.
Should be in opera not a roustabout!

The kookaburra singing in our ears,
We trip-toe to the van.  My swag unzips
Itself beside the Digger.  Spew in tears
From slouch hat down inverted rifle drips.
Saluting, swaying I retreat to sleep —
Fishing for Barramundi with Rough Seas
Off **Mornington** — We cast into the deep,
And strike trevally, but no lure can please
That hump-back king to rise.

                          Some time we can't
Get what we want.
                  He smiles.
                       You sly old fraud.
You know each fish up here by name!
                    I rant,
But still, we catch not one.  Later, aboard,
I open up his gift and find the fish
In ochre on a piece of bark.  A flash
Beyond us leaps, an angler's glimmering wish
Which shimmies, splits the ocean with a splash.

The kettle's whistle cleaves my crowbarred head,
The digger's baleful gaze pierces with light
The haze of hops.  She gongs to wake the dead,
Bonging a billy but we have no bite.
Only slewed sluicing with a cold tap douche
Succeeds.  Hot coffee speeds us plus cold toast
To thick-tongued parting, dumps me legless, louche
And feckless in Gomorrah, the Gold Coast. . . .

# Canto 8

A cruising Jaguar picks up my trails —
Weary, flat and sweaty, stale.  An old bloke —
White shoes, shorts and towelling hat — prevails
On me to join him.
                     You look fagged, son.  Poke
Your ruck sack in the back and park your bum.
I'm for **Mackay**, to find the Marlin boat
This bankrupt bookie owes me.  Where d'you come
From then?
              Near **Cairns**.  I need to be afloat
Up on the Gulf next week.  You got a drink?

In twenty miles I know this great hotel
That's stuck right on the beach, whaddaya think?

(I'd suck a boxer's sponge after the bell
My throat's so dry, but there's the rub.)
                          OK —
Stopping my gob with my last butter-scotch
I say —
First round my shout, take it away
Then James!

              I try to not look at my watch —
No cruise-control but still the speedo sticks
On 56 Imperial miles an hour.
I ask him how and why as my tongue licks
My lips.  He smiles,

          Common-sense: best use of power
For torque, for best economy of fuel.

(As wayward words can helter-skelter burn
The roof right off your mouth, a one-way duel
Above the limit with no lane to turn,
Locked steering wheel, no gears and worn out brakes

Skidding into silence, I lock my jaw)
The sweet melts in my mouth, the driver takes
A turn down a dirt track and finds the shore:

One of the best kept secrets up this way
This pub, cheap rooms and tucker too!!

                             The hiss
Of Four-X opening on the Moreton Bay
Fig shaded promontory, the cold beer's kiss
Fondling my throat beside the wasp-free sea,
The frangipani perfume wafting waves
Up to the hotel's stilted balcony
All justify his tourist brochure raves.
Thalassa, thalassa, tears sear my eyes.
He watches as I plunge in jeans and all.
A pile of stubbies joins me and he lies
Beer-bellied on the sand.  The flip tops fall
And I make motorbikes from them in chains,
(We drink the doldrums in the Gulf that way)
And listen, for nothing beside remains
Except his voice.

                    When we were kids they'd pay
Us ten bob a fox, down by **Lake Tyers**,
Beyond the pale, in "Caledonia
Australis," as Gippsland was.  Then bush fires
Burnt down the school, beggared my father
In the year of the crash, when charcoaled sheep
Stood in the paddocks waiting to be clubbed.
When Mum died in an op, nothing could keep
Him off the booze.  Huh . . . One night we both blubbed
When he'd whistled the stock whip round our ears
Like a stockman cracking a black snake's back.
Then we were packed off to an aunt's for years
Of half-cast housekeepers and mouldy tack.
They told us stories of a figure-head
Found washed up on the beach after a wreck,
A pale white Venus, sent back from the dead:

She was buried in sand up to her neck . . .
When Dad had drunk us dry the bank foreclosed.
A Jaguar rolled up the drive, a "Swell"
From South Yarra strolled our verandah, posed
And left his after-shave for us to smell.
Then I ran off, worked in a timber mill.
I swore I'd have a car like that.  I found
My fingers loved machines — they tinkered till
They built a buzz-saw worth two thousand pound.
A factory next to turn out drills and tools
For **Broken Hill**.  Artillery shells made
Me a million in the War.  The dribbling fools
In Toorak snub me still — I never played
By their school rules.  I found when I went back
Blacks squatting on our farm, the soil choked
With salt.  To find our graves I had to hack
Away the weeds.  At my old school I poked
About while spotty calves played hop-scotch.
Then when  . . .
                    he fell asleep, I carefully laid
Him in the Jag and drove, the sun a blotch
On the left hand page of the sky.  He stayed
Out cold until Mackay.  I know the name
Of his hotel and leave him parked there, tramp
To curlewed dark beyond the neon flame.
A ballyhooly's shelter is my camp.


Among the rats I fall asleep at last
And in my head the rogue white elephants
Circle on the roundabout of the past,
Shaped and turned with me on the lathe of chance
To bugle and blunder along with the herd
Bewildered, through forests, tangled with thorns,
Trampling the nest of the gold humming bird
Which sips the nectar of the future, warns
Of the stakes in the pit beneath the grass;
But her song is not heard amid the din,
As the elephants plunge I cry, can brass
Wake up a trumpet, wood a violin?

# Canto 10

I roll out the other side of **Bowen**
Where the sun bowls right over the flame trees
In a scalding northerly breeze.  Once shown
The way I loiter till an Alpha frees
Me from the end of my tether.  Her face
Is strangely familiar: long dark tresses
Coil about her head, memory racks to trace
The potpourri which clasps and caresses
Me, dips a madelaine in coconut
And lime and drapes me in the sari wrapped
Around her waist.  Her smile opens doors shut
Long ago:

       Hello . . . Lots of strays get snapped
Up on this road . . . For once I'll break the rule:
You look O.K. . . . A bit done in maybe,
But not the type . . . still, who can tell.  The fool-
ish thing is, I couldn't care less . . . Crazy,
But it's a fair way yet to **Innisfail** —
Go on, earn your ride.  Tell me a story,
Doesn't matter what.

           Words change tack, sail
Out of anchorage looking for glory
In yarns, some true: they make me the raw prawn —
She laughs at skipping sea snakes the net dumps
On the deck when it breaks, sits quiet when dawn
Dips its pink fingers in Torres Strait, jumps
As Skip. treads on a Stone Fish, swims away
On the tide with a Mermaid (Dugong) when
We reach her turn off.  She asks me to stay,
Tells me her name . . . Penelope.  Open
Sesame garden splashed with lorikeet
And spangled drongo.  Azure kingfishers
Strobe in blue a jungled rainforest retreat,
A home to answer every painter's wishes.

Her canvasses surpass John Walker's best
**Port Douglas** works.  The colours glow.  She tells
Me she admires Rothko, his endless quest
For hues of icons, frescos to make bells
Ring in your eye.

                  I'm never satisfied:
I gloss over tints from the day before
Or toss the whole thing in the bin . . .  I tried
To find out why . . .

              And then we spoke no more.

JOHN WATSON

# TO MARIANNE MOORE

There are still a few of us left for whom
Inverted commas, floating like Mickey Mouse ears
Of cress over the rye bread of a line of verse,
Inevitably recall Pound's *Mauberley*;
For instance if, as in a trance, I chance upon
"Gloxinias were to him a 'button-hole'"
The distinguishing marks, like masts seen first
Over the horizon of a Sargasso Sea,
Suggest his "to maintain 'the sublime'"
Or his "fundamental passion," his "true Penelope . . ."
Others, no doubt, confronted by the device,
As ornamental as a wrought-iron gryphon,
(An image for you, O Artificer of my youthful memories)
Would think always of its captivating misuse
As in the greengrocer's "Fresh" "Fruit" or "Genuine" "Reductions."
Fowler, of course, dismisses almost every instance
Of their concessional use to the rubric *Superiority*
Implying "If you need to use them then you shouldn't,"
And vice-versa.  But you, O Maid Marianne
Of the mysterious Sherwood Forest of our adolescence
Where, in the amiable light of affectionate recall,
Your meticulous ease animated the anthologies —
You introduced us to the idiom of the block
Quotation spilling and spreading, travelling along
"Over hill, over dale" for several meandering lines
Like a stately ice-berg being towed to somewhere
Hot and strange and dry and anchoring in its harbour
Meltingly to attract such native amazement
As would animate all its crowded foreshores.
And on occasions you contrived the same
Curious ability to leap with aplomb
And soar from the page as do the words *I love you*
In the facsimile letters of Wallis Simpson.

The invention of specifics!  For all of us
Who sensed that it was something marginal
That everyone was hoping could be said,
You wheeled into our library the tray-mobile
With an afternoon-tea of *Scientific Americans.*
One knew instinctively that one was in the presence
Of poetry on being told "Reindeer are over-serious"
And in similar pronouncements quite beyond Cartesian doubt,
The facts were not in dispute, merely the alignment of the barrel
Which pointed unexpectedly towards some portion of the woods
Where no-one else had thought to look.
                    There we saw,
At a garden table of dolomite, groups of dreamers
Like Alice and the Hatter, conversing in as cogent
A manner as they, while someone's radio
Disturbed the poplar air with a baritone's
*When the morning glory wakes up in the morning,*
*Then I'll kiss your tu-lips goodnight*
And from an adjoining table in deep shade
A voice declaiming from a magazine
Something we had always longed to hear,
As hard and beautiful as granite about to be carved,
"I say sometimes to Isabelle Adjani
*Our life is a wall and each film is a stone.*
She always says *That is not true*
*Each film is the wall . . ."*
                    And then
In the shadow of a cactus wing
Someone is talking of Cocteau's famous answer —
Asked the hoary question *If your house were on fire*
*What would you take if you could take just one thing?*
He had said *"I'd take the fire."*
And you, O mistress of the inventory,
You would take the arsonist's address
And call for tea and note the pattern on the tablecloth
And see the weir shining through the window
Like a benevolent lamp out-of-doors.

If life were just such images!  Or facts!
Rather than the perplexities of spreading them
Unfolded on a vast and dappled table where
To think this sufficient is to be taken aback
And to find that what is needed is instead
A sculptural fanfare, a walking presence, an immersion;
But you, O Celebrant of the aardvark's emotions,
You, Keeper of the Seals (the ones slipping
From ice-floes into the dark striated flood)
You managed always to enter the parting stream,
To swim towards the falls and the salmon's pool
While standing still beside it, gazing orthogonally
Across its demanding surfaces, contented
Like Jefferson looking with pride at evening
Towards Monticello.  Smilingly you achieved
In images like waterlilies tied
But floating in the tide "reality removed
But reality nonetheless because we know
It is removed," a formidable mystery — this fact,
That you attained the facility "to proceed
From one thing to another crossing all gaps
Regardless but keeping them in mind."  And O
The rapid and lovely intrusion, like water
Entering water at a weir or junction or lock,
Of your quotations marking their ruffle and wake
Like Horowitz's doubled octaves in *Pictures
From an Exhibition* and with the same
Good-natured, almost monumental, high seriousness.

Another mystery you noted which makes the world
Go round like a perpetual-motion machine
Endlessly weighted with inequalities,
Is the odd and curious co-existence, in a world
Of useful and functional entities, of things
(Pure gold exposed by the plough's chance grazing)
Themselves symbols of the mysteries, expressive of them
*Simply in themselves* without interpretative grace
For instance *the flame* which already is at least
To some degree unphysical, or white *water*

Taken to a high place and let fall, the waterfall
In which opacity is the result of fractures . . .
That such elusive things should inhere
Side by side with the furniture of this world!
Such elemental mysteries as opposed to those
Of ceremony or decree, you, O artificer
Of the natural world, you ensured always
Were just round the corner of the next path
Of the next calm banquet of pointed comment
As if you were delivering the speech of congratulations
Which greeted the first conquerors of Everest
At the very moment of their breathless arrival
And had been waiting all morning for them to reach you,
Reading and pencilling marginal notes.
The apotheosis of that compulsive
"Because-it-is-there," your poetry glistens
Like that clear glacial air — "I can see no reason
For calling my work poetry except that there is
No other category into which to put it."

Suggestions of all-inclusiveness pervade
Your *Pangolin,* for instance, as if for something to exist
It must combine, with all its primary qualities
Such as define its essence, something more —
Spray from an ocean of adjoining worlds
Qualities which were not its alone
But which it shares communally —
Recalling the Brassai photograph of Bonnard
As an old man, painting several paintings at once
On a single piece of canvas tacked to the wall.
The poem is of course a means of engaging
The attention of the dreamer at the canal
Who otherwise beguiled by the little weir
Might well believe that nothing else exists.
With text in hand he holds a lens unfocussing
And fixative; the weir is suddenly
Resplendent with these simultaneities
And *everything* by implication with *all else*
Lingers and clings to him like a net —

Just as Renoir's brother used to ask the passers-by
Beside a bridge across the adjoining Seine,
Idle and puzzling questions to detain them
While his brother painted them in deft strokes.

My purpose in coming to this abandoned quarry
Is "opaque through being fractured"
By shafts of affection like light through clouds.
In such a place so strongly shaped by the past
Extraction of its granite blocks
Where core-samples of the stone lie scattered
Like cylinders of salt some sculptor might
Have once brought back to forward-looking life,
The air is still with ancient glances.
One senses everywhere core-samples of events.
Here one could expect to find a vast repository
Of scrolls — of recollections, messages, accounts;
Like the ancient Egyptian missive concerning chick-peas
Quoted by Gower as a model of economy
Of expression, or childish games and riddles
Like that involving the story of the three wells
With its deliciously irreducible reply *Well Well Well.*
In the air the scrolls unfold proclaiming
"A replicating D.N.A. of images." It is then
I know that you are here. A curtain
Of last-recorded words is mixed with afternoon light:
"All my possessions for a moment in time"
And "They couldn't hit the side of a barn at this
Distance," and even (that chestnut) "What is the question?"
The sun showed no sign of setting
Despite its having travelled several times
Below the trees in the darkening quarry;
I could not read the variousness of these scrolls
Without the Rosetta-stone of your inventions:
For you found amongst the strewn dross
Of an intriguingly "finite but unbounded" quarry
Pebbles out of which to make a garden bower
And paths, like a plait coiled round a Medici head,
Which might happily negotiate

The thickets and avenues and hidden lakes
Of your improvisatory style, its quotations
Possibly, in your view, "disruptive of pleasant progress"
Yet pursued with a passion equalling that of the following:
"She is the only actress to have made me cry
In front of a television screen and so I wanted
To film her and so steal precious things
From her — for instance every single thing
The face expresses in its transformations"
(The mysterious vagueness of translation!) —
A garden bower in which we sit again
To a tea made entirely of the marvellous.